A few
words

A few
words

LAURENCE F. McNAMEE, PH.D.
and
KENT BIFFLE

Taylor Publishing Company
Dallas, Texas

Published by Taylor Publishing Company
              1550 West Mockingbird Lane
              Dallas, Texas 75235

Library of Congress Cataloging-in-Publication Data

McNamee, Laurence F.
    A few words / by Laurence F. McNamee and Kent Biffle.
        p.   cm.
    "Columns included in this collection originally appeared in the
Dallas morning news"—T.p. verso.
    ISBN 0-87833-615-X (pbk.) : $14.95
    1. English philology.   2. English language—Etymology.
3. Americanisms.   I. Biffle, Kent.   II. Title.
PE27.M36   1988
422—dc19   88-10184
                                                                  CIP

Printed in the United States of America

10 9 8 7 6 5 4 3 2 1

to
Bob Compton

Foreword

Otto Eduard Leopold von Bismarck, Germany's Iron Chancellor, observed that the factor most influencing the course of the nineteenth century was that the same language was spoken by the British and the Americans.

If we assume for a moment that the British and the Americans do speak the same language, we must still question whether the perceptive Bismarck or any nineteenth-century clairaudient could have foretold how influential English would become in the twentieth century.

In our time, English—out of 8,000 languages—has become the premier language of the entire world.

Visionary though he was, the old Prussian could not have dreamed that 700,000,000 people would be speaking English—and arguing about its use and raising questions about its origins and structure. He could not, in other words, have anticipated a book of this sort.

How and when did this language start? What was the first poem written in this tongue? Who was its greatest author (Shakespeare, right?) and what was the secret of his power? What was there about the language of Shakespeare that could reach over the footlights and gather up an audience? How did we get so many Latin words in a language that was basically Germanic? What was the vernacular spoken by the knights at the Round Table? In what language were the *Sonnets From the Portuguese* first written?

In this book the reader will find answers to queries sufficiently searching to plow furrows in academic brows (split infinitives to pluperfect subjunctives) and questions airy enough to delight trivia pursuers (platonic to Platonic). What's a "chunnel" in Britain? A "posslq" in the USA?

Such are the mysteries that Professor Laurence McNamee, an academician, and Kent Biffle, a journalist, have been addressing in *The Dallas Morning News* for many years. This selection from their columns appears here in book form for the first time. Any questions?

Jim Lehrer
Co-anchor, PBS-TV's *MacNeil-Lehrer Newshour,* and
author of *Kick the Can.*

Contents

Authors' Note

"Unprovided with original learning, unformed in the habits of thinking, unskilled in the arts of composition, I decided to write a book."
—Edward Gibbon

A little over a decade ago, a young professor was touring Texas penal institutions with a troupe of Shakespearean actors. When Don King, the boxing promoter, heard of the venture, he wanted to join up, especially when he learned that the actors found convicts their best audience and that the inmates themselves found their greatest catharsis in an evening of Shakespeare. "Maybe there's a resonant chord somewhere," Don wrote to the professor. "After all, no one can express the polarities of life the way Shakespeare can, and no one has experienced these polarities as deeply as these men—love and hate, life and death. I need to coordinate my schedule with yours so I can join up as an M/C or a bit player."

Now here was a news feature second only to "man bites dog." So the professor immediately contacted the *Dallas Morning News.* It wasn't just that Don King had once been a "guest" at Marion State Institute of Correction; it was there that he had begun his studies in Shakespeare. It wasn't just that he had been interested in "escape" literature; here was a man who could recite entire pages of Shakespeare verbatim. "I came out armed with knowledge," says King.

Somehow, our promoter never was able to perform before this captive audience (something about the return of Muhammad Ali); but during the correspondence between the professor and his contact at the *News,* the suggestion came up that they start a *Dear Abby* column on language. "We get questions on grammar every week that we can't answer," the editor of the book section confessed. As soon as *A Few Words* emerged as a regular Sunday column, the questions began to increase in arithmetical progression and now threaten to take on a progression that is geometrical.

Readers also began to suggest an anthology. "Sometimes I'm out of town and miss your column. Why don't youse guys do a book?" So we did. And we owe the initiatory step to a guy who used to sell numbers on the streets of Cleveland.

Every book is the result of the combined efforts of many people; the guy on the dust jacket is merely the entrepreneur. And since there are two of us, our debts are deep and double. Never has so small a work incurred such a heavy load of indebtedness. Yet there are three whom we should mention for special plaudits, each from a disparate discipline: the aforementioned promoter, an editor, and an official in charge of eviction notices.

Don King we have mentioned and thank profusely. The next person to whom we are indebted to is our editor at Taylor Publishing Company, Jim Donovan. He pioneered the project and established an orderly arrangement from an amorphous mass of heterogeneous material. The reader will note how the book starts with Language in General ("How did languages start?"), becomes more narrow with The English Language ("How many people speak English?"), and much more narrow in Chapter Three, Regional English ("What's the story on 'y'all' in Texas and the Valley Girl language in California?") Subsequent chapters focalize further as our tome addresses syntax, spelling, and punctuation. For his organizing skill in bringing cosmos out of chaos, we raise a glass to him.

The last thank you goes to the official who issued our "eviction" notice. Due to a technicality, we were forced to vacate our office in a hurry, and in the process our extensive file of "Emendations"—corrections, questions, corroborations, and amplifications from our readers—was lost, stolen, or strayed. Without the need to incorporate this material, the book was finished even quicker than expected. And when the Emendations do surface, they will furnish the nucleus of Volume II.

It remains for us to acknowledge our source of support. It would take more than a few words for us to express our gratitude to the many readers who have sent us questions and to the many who read the answers. Thank you one and all.

Kent Biffle & Laurence McNamee

I.

Language in general

Q: Like all public officials, I find that what I mean to say is not always what people hear me say. This situation leads me to wonder about the origin and development of language. How did it develop? Why?

A. Starke Taylor
Mayor of Dallas
Dallas, TX

A: There are many theories, so many that the linguistic Society of Paris once passed a resolution outlawing any further discussion of the topic. Of all the theories, the oldest is the MYSTICAL.

In the tranquillity of the Garden of Eden, our first parents assigned a name to everything, at God's direction. "Let's call it an elephant, Eve; it looks like an elephant." A similar theory was later advocated by Plato; only in this case it was not God but a legislator who gave a natural name to everything.

Centuries later, in the intellectual ferment of the university, Professor Max Mueller challenged the MYSTICAL theory while advocating his own BOW-WOW theory. "Language grew out of man's attempt to duplicate natural sounds," he elucidated. In other words, just as a child refers to a cow as a *moo-moo* and to a train as a *choo-choo,* so primitive man developed onomatopeiac words for *bump, buzz, thunder*—words that echo the sound.

So far so good until this BOW-WOW theory was pooh-poohed by another professor who queried why it would *thunder* in Galveston but over in Guadalajara it would *tonar;* why bees would *buzz* in Beaumont but *zumm* in Zufenhausen. "Speech originated from the spontaneous overflowing of powerful feeling, cries of pain, cries of joy, cries of fear," according to the POOH-POOH theory.

"No, no, no, the primitive chants that developed during the early ritualistic dances had nothing to do with fear of pain," said another professor as he advocated his SING-SONG theory. "Is it not much more logical to assume that language evolved from the chants that accompany dance, the ritualistic dance?"

"How ridiculous! Who said that primitive man had time to dance? He was working; he was doing hard work," pontificated a professor of anthropology as he advocated his YO-HE-YO theory. "I must postulate that language evolved from grunts, gasps, glottal contractions—utterances evoked by strenuous physical exertions while, say, dragging a log, or moving a pyramid."

These are the five most popular theories over which learned professors have quibbled and squabbled: MYSTICAL, BOW-WOW, POOH-POOH, SING-SONG, and YO-HE-YO. Put them all together and you won't get change for a nickel because none of them touch on the role played by the mind of man in the development of a concept language. We simply do not know. Although our age has seen many languages die, it has never seen one develop from the gestation period: written records go back less than six thousand years while this creature man has been around for over six million. We simply do not know, despite the volubility of pontificating professors.

So much for the *how;* as to the *why,* the scholars are strangely silent. Not so the politicians, who generally go down the line with the politically adept Maurice de Talleyrand: "Language was given to us so that we may conceal our thoughts."

* * *

One of the local rabbis offered an amendment to the above: "Although we have never seen a language develop from the gestation period, our age has witnessed the resurrection of one that was dead—Hebrew."

Q: While growing up in Binghampton, New York, I learned Lithuanian, English, and Polish at the same time, and though I never confused the three while speaking them, I did notice many things that were the same about them, similarities.

Later, in my travels as a sailor and a professional athlete, I began to see that there were many items the same in just about every European language. The only language that seemed completely on its own was the one spoken by Paulino Uzcudun; but then Paulino gave everybody trouble, except Joe Louis.

I once thought of examining the relationship of my native Lithuanian with Sanskrit but never got around to it. Reporters always advised me to stick to boxing.

> Jack Sharkey
> Epping, NH

A: Our answer to any question by a former heavyweight champion is always a resounding "yes."

But to elaborate a little, we'd point out that the phenomenon you refer to is the Indo-European language tree. Indo-European was a language spoken during the Stone Age and seems to be the common ancestor of the languages of India, Iran, and all the European countries with two exceptions. One of these is the Basque language spoken by your colleague, Paulino Uzcudun. The Grimm brothers (yes, the fairy tale Grimms) did a lot of research on the origin and structure of the Indo-European language. Subsequent researchers have placed its home in Lithuania.

Your observation about Lithuania and Sanskrit is most apt. Although India and Lithuania were separated by several thousand miles, their languages (Sanskrit and Lithuanian) both preserved many old features (though not always the same ones) that have practically disappeared from other languages of the Indo-European family tree. Until recently, Lithuanian peasants could understand many phrases and sentence patterns of Sanskrit.

Had you continued your interest, you would have made a contribution to the study of language, but the sports world would have lost a colorful performer.

* * *

On noting our reference to the Grimm brothers, Professor Joseph Littlejohn of Southeastern Oklahoma State in Durant suggested that sometime we do a column on Grimm's Law and ". . . explain why so many words that begin with the letter *p* in Latin emerged in English with the letter *f:* piscis-fish; pater-father; pes-foot."

We promised to oblige but first had to answer a question on the number of languages in the world.

Q: How many languages are there in the world, how many can one learn, and what is the average time it takes to learn a language? I am a native of Spain with a degree in English and look forward to a career as a translator or teacher.

Maria Wagnon
Denton, TX

A: Some experts say that there are 3,000 languages in the world; others guesstimate it as high as 8,000. But nobody can determine the exact number because more than half of the languages have never been codified into a formal grammar—they are merely spoken.

No one, of course, has ever learned all 3,000, but the linguistic attainments of a few talented individuals are astonishing and perhaps unduplicable.

August Wilhelm Von Schlegel (1767–1845) knew English, Italian, and Spanish so well that he was able to pen the definitive translations of Shakespeare, Dante, and Calderon, and still have time to practice his Icelandic and Sanskrit.

Another German, Heinrich Schliemann (1822–1900), memorized two novels in the first foreign language he studied and continued to memorize two novels in every subsequent language—18 in all.

Cardinal Giuseppi Mezzofanti (1774–1849) had only a minor interest in novels, and no interest in travel (he never left Italy), yet he was able to speak 40 languages fluently, 30 passably, and could "get by" in 45 additional dialects.

Being born down under in New Zealand did not hamper the linguistic aptitude of Harold Whitmore Williams (1876–1928), as he went on to develop fluency in 28 languages and adequacy in 52 others. Rumor has it that he learned one of the Balkan languages within 48 hours.

The most prodigious polyglot of all times was Sir John Bowring (1792–1872). His lordship could read in 200 different languages and *parlez-vous* in 100. If they had had language labs in those days, a guy like that could have learned a new one every week.

How many languages can a language major learn? That question is difficult to answer because none of the above ever elected to "major" in language. Schlegel was a professor of literary criticism; the Cardinal, a prefect at the Vatican library; Williams, an editor; Bowring, a diplomat; and Schliemann, a businessman who dabbled in archaeology long enough to discover the site of ancient Troy.

Since you are interested in a translating career, may we advise you to eschew Alaskan Eyak. It is spoken by only two people. But you will be able to touch base with two billion if you concentrate on your native Spanish, your adopted English, along with Chinese, Russian, and Hindi. It may surprise you to learn that there are only 30 languages in the world which are spoken by more than a million people.

How long does it take to master a language? A modern philologist, Dr. Margaret McClear, once answered that succinctly: "To acquire a few tongues is the task of a few years; to be eloquent in one is the labor of a lifetime."

Q: Why are Americans so weak in foreign language? As district sales-manager, I'm continually frustrated when I try to recruit bilingual salesmen, and it's getting worse.

Tony Mandina
Houston, TX

A: The explanation revolves around geography, history, and pedagogy. To begin with, geography has its way of imposing its own reality upon a nation. With an English-speaking neighbor to the north and two sprawling oceans on our flanks, there was little economic incentive for a foreign language program to develop in our country. Whenever a translator was needed, there were plenty of recent immigrants, and Americans adopted an insolent, insular attitude: "Let 'em learn English." After all, who had the sound currency, the mighty military, the huge industrial potential?

But all of this is in the past: "Sic transit gloria mundi."

The problem got worse during the sixties. Under pressure from activists, many college administrators deleted language from the curriculum in favor of "relevant" courses. And in order to attract students during the '70s, all but 8 percent of the colleges dropped their language entrance requirements, and only a paucity retain language as a graduation requirement.

Always good for a laugh is the rejoinder: "In college I studied 'Beginning Japanese' but in Japan nobody wanted to speak 'Beginning Japanese.'" Unfortunately, our trade deficit is no laughing matter. There are more than 10,000 meticulously tailored Japanese salesmen in the United States selling their Japanese products—all in flawless English. We have fewer than a thousand such counterparts: we started too late; we pay teachers too little; and most college administrators are too hostile to language programs.

So barring a miracle or a magical mañana, we can expect to see our trade deficit get worse and worse.

Q: When Mel Tillis gives his TV commercials, he stutters; however, when he sings, everything is perfect, not a trace of stuttering. I've noticed this proclivity among some of my associates. What's the reason?

Marcella Booth
Storrs, CT

A: It goes back to the twofold division within the brain. The left half controls language, while music is assigned to the right. When we switch from one mental process to the other, we also shift hemispheres, according to Professor Jon Jonz, a language specialist.

The professor informs us, although we had not asked, that anyone can master a foreign language without a trace of an accent simply by beginning the study *before* the two halves of the brain specialize.

Regrettably for the cause of bilingual education, this specialization is completed between the ages of four to six, *before* one normally starts to school. True, there are notable exceptions, but from the age of six upwards any linguistic acquisition is in the same league as plastic surgery. It rarely becomes part of you, and for that reason adults have diminished chances of becoming truly bilingual. But with the kids, they are linguistic chameleons and not only learn a foreign language quicker but also better.

Q: "How did the kitty turn his motor on?" is a question that elementary children ask when they hear a cat purr. Could you tell us? Is it a belly voice?

Eleanor Clark
Carver Elementary
Greenville, TX

A: Cats purr with their vocal cords. One cord purrs on inhaling, the other on exhaling. The mechanism developed, according to scientists, to enable the mother cat to soothe her frightened kittens. In the 18th century, Dr. Samuel Johnson found the purring not only soothing but inspiring and, whenever possible, would do his writing near a purring puss.

Q: Why do people use profanity? My husband, who is a voice professor, told me they use it because of poverty of vocabulary. Yet the most ear-blistering profanity I ever heard came from an English professor who taught a course in vocabulary improvement. Surely my husband can't be wrong. Gene is always right.

Mrs. Doris Feuchtinger
Semmes, AL

A: A philologist and pedant would answer first by pointing to the essential relationship between profanity and that which is holy. The word comes from the Latin ("pro" and "fanum") which means "outside the temple."

He would then distinguish between the profanity in Catholic countries, where religious tradition produced expletives loaded with blasphemies, and the profanity in Puritan countries, where certain words about defecation and urination were considered naughty because of religious taboos regarding any mention of bodily functions. The Puritan is scatological; the Catholic, eschatological.

A psychologist might explain profanity as an emotional safety valve, characteristic of all human groups, ancient and modern. Profanity's effectiveness as an emotional release might be questioned, however, by anyone who has heard a man cuss out his ulcer.

A moralist might claim that most profanity may not be profanity at all because it has become habitual in its use by so many people. Ironically, for example, you may have heard an unthinking mother refer to her offspring as a mean S.O.B.

Those who savor the flavor of profanity might cite the cussing skills of Francois Rabelais, Mark Twain, Harry S. Truman, Ernest Hemingway, and poet-novelist James Dickey, each an artist with words. They might hypothesize that perhaps there just aren't any other words that express the full range of feelings of such writers.

On the other hand, those who object to profanity might point out that each of these writers rebelled against his upbringing. Twain, for example, was exposed early to strict Presbyterianism.

As to our opinion, we think the voice professor has a valid point, although ***** we hate like hell to admit it!

* * *

Dr. Pat Pope of Garland writes to remind us of a passage in the play *Inherit the Wind*, where Darrow tells William Jennings Bryant, "there are very few words in the English language that everybody understands and we ought to use every damned one of them."

Q: *What is dyslexia and what can be done about it? Is it inherited, as some say, or is it due to brain damage? At one time, we identified it with poverty and illiteracy, but lately it seems to be showing up in the middle class also.*

Mary Ann Williams
Eight Mile, AL

A: Dyslexia is no respecter of classes. Little Nelson had to be sent to a special school in Manhattan because of this ailment and was hampered his entire life by problems in reading. His daughter once confided, ". . . in the evenings when our family would read the Bible aloud we always had to skip Daddy." Nevertheless, Nelson Rockefeller was able to attain the vice presidency of the United States. Another dyslexic, Woodrow Wilson, even though he was unable to read till age eleven, went one step higher.

Those who succeed do so because early in life they learned how to compensate. For example, George Patton learned how to beat the system by memorizing everything verbatim. It always worked, except the time he failed math in his plebe year at West Point and the time he tried to memorize the alphabet: "I always have trouble with A, B, and what do you call that other letter?" It's hard to believe but Albert Einstein was plagued with the problem of transposing numbers and was still encountering problems in basic arithmetic the very year he propounded his theory of relativity.

Time was when both psychologists and elementary teachers would attribute dyslexia to brain damage and automatically send kids home as "hopelessly addled." Some, rejected and dejected, went home to vegetate. But one of these rejects went home and invented the light bulb. Thomas Edison also developed the movie camera, the phonograph, and 1,090 other innovative machines and devices. Others in this syndrome were artists like Rodin, Nobel-prize winner Paul Ehrlich, Prime Minister Winston Churchill of Britain, Harvard President A. L. Lowell, physicist Niels Bohr, brain surgeon Harvey Cushing, and a considerable number of literary luminaries including Hans Christian Andersen, Gustave Flaubert, William Butler Yeats, and Amy Lowell.

Unlike celibacy, dyslexia can be inherited, and for reasons no one knows is generally transmitted through female genes. Equally puzzling is the fact that fewer women are afflicted than males, although psychiatrists attribute this paucity to the fact that maturation takes place earlier in females.

By definition, dyslexia is simply a disorder that causes the victim difficulty in reading, speaking, spelling, and writing. Sometimes he confuses letters that are similar and he frequently transposes letters. With numbers, he may write that 3×5 is 51 while knowing that the correct answer is 15. The sooner the problem is attacked, the better. If the child receives proper attention in the first grade, there is an 80 percent chance of recovery; by the end of the third grade, the betting odds dip to 43 percent.

Re-training the pupil in language units starts by clarifying the visual and auditory patterns and then—this is important—strengthening the linkage of the visual and auditory with the motor elements of speech and writing. Progress moves with gazelle-like speed if the pupil can see tangible results, such as academic victories. As new research continues, there is also some hope for victims of this troublesome affliction.

From Pat Machen of Rockwall, Texas, we learn that dyslexics generally have very high social intelligence. Also that, for some unknown reason, they do very well in Latin and algebra.

Q: I need your help on two phrases that are appearing with increasing frequency in press and magazines as well as on TV and radio. Please publish your thoughts on these for all to see.

First is "it seems . . ." It seems that hardly any writer or speaker can get started without using this. "IT SEEMS that this man. . . ." or "IT SEEMS that once upon a time . . ." Does proper usage frown on beginning a sentence with plain, direct "Two Irishmen . . ." or "Once upon a time . . ."?

Philip Brady
Denton, TX

A: The phrase about the legendary Irishmen can be classified as an "opener," a legitimate stylistic device and as necessary as the exposition of a play.

Romeo and Juliet doesn't begin with a boy-meets-girl scene, not even with Romeo or Juliet, but with a feud, the force that will prove fatal to the hero. All this—the feud, the unique hero, the youthful heroine—are part of the exposition, the opener.

In conversation there are many such openers. "In those days a decree went forth from Caesar Augustus" prepares the reader for a solemn event of historic importance.

"A funny thing happened to me on the way to the studio" establishes a mood of frivolity.

"It seems that two Irishmen" wafts us into the land of reminiscence and speculation with a puckish touch of make-believe. Although a trifle overdone of late, it is as legitimate an opener as the British "Oh, say, there, old bloke."

Not so with "at this point in time."

The following analogy will demonstrate. "At a distant point in time, ice-cream manufacturers discovered they could increase their profits by a simple expedient: pumping air into ice cream. And the lower the quality of the ice cream, the greater their profits—until legislators coerced them to sell their stuff not by bulk but by weight.

"But a sweet lesson was learned on the way to the legislature. The lawmakers themselves also began to pump air, more air, into their already overblown language."

The lower the thought content, the more pompous the language—and the greater the opportunity to say nothing—and mean it!

During the Watergate period "at this point in time" became a point in pain that has lingered.

Misuse of words is regrettable because it is the misuse of man's greatest gift, the miracle of language.

After all, without language how could one cuss people who go around saying "at this point in time"?

II.

The English Language

Q: In what part of the United States is the best English spoken? Back in our native land, the best German is spoken in Berlin (and Hanover), and our cousins in England tell us that London is the home of the King's English. However, none of the people down at the local feed store sound like Laurence Olivier.

Albert, Frieda, and Siegfried Feucht
Paris, TX

A: Ever since Adam invited Eve to "come over to my place and see my etchings" the speech of mankind has taken on individual peculiarities. But no particular language can claim to be the "best" language, nor can any dialect within a language claim to be the superior dialect.

True, in many countries there is a prestige dialect, the one used by political leaders and the upper class. This is the dialect that is taught in the schools and propagated by the media. It is also the dialect that is spoken in the political or cultural center of the respective country: Berlin, London, Paris, etc. The one exception is the United States, and for several reasons—our country is younger, our population is more mobile, and the media is all pervasive.

At one time it was thought that a Boston accent was the best social artillery, especially during the flowering of New England and the heyday of Harvard. But the vaunted "superiority" of the Boston accent was always something social and was never accepted by any philologist worth his salt, nor by the morning performers on soap operas or the evening stars of TV who consistently employ Standard American English (SAE). In fact, the so-called network standard is based on the Inland North dialects typical of the Chicago area. If a generalization will be pardoned, Standard American English is spoken in every part of the United States except in New England and in the Deep South (which includes Texas).

This is one reason your friends at the feed store don't sound like Sir Laurence Olivier: they are speaking the Southern dialect.

We suggest that if you are going to travel to other parts of the United States, you try to get hooked on soap operas; however, if you're going to remain in the Lone Star State, study your verbs, prepositions, and propositions down at the local feed store.

Q: While traveling in the Third World, I am continually amazed at the linguistic ability of the people we once considered "savages." It will surprise many Americans to learn that most people in Africa speak two or

*three languages. Frequently, one of those languages is English. And this is
my question. How many people in the world speak English?*

*Archie Moore
The Third World*

A: English is the first language of 400 million people and the second
language of another 300 million. As you note, quite a few of those 300
million live in Africa, for it is one of the official languages of Nigeria and
Uganda and an unofficial language in many of the developing countries
where native languages compete for primacy.

English is used throughout the world by airline personnel, financiers,
and diplomats. It surpasses any rival language including Chinese, which,
though spoken by 900 million Chinese, is rarely used by non-Chinese. We
can be proud of our hard-working language. It's a knockout.

And, speaking of knockouts, we're always glad to oblige a former
heavyweight champ with 141 KOs to his record.

*Q: How did we get so many Latin words in the English language? My
friend says they came through the holy Church, but I suspect they came
through those mean Romans.*

A: Both of you are right, up to a point. Caesar and his legions, St. Augustine and his missionaries—both groups enriched the Anglo-Saxon
language with Latin derivatives. One thing the Romans did was to build a
lot of camps wherever they conquered; and since the roman word *castra*
(camp) came into our language as *chester,* the preponderance of such
place-names as Leicester, Lancaster, and Dorchester gives evidence not
only to the large number of Roman camps but also to their influence
upon our language. Every time your uncle in Rochester puts Worcester
sauce on his dog Chester's Alpo helper, they both demonstrate their indebtedness to the Roman occupation of England.

As for the Church, it brought in certain ecclesiastical terms like *angel*
and *candle* (*angelus, candela*) and academic words like *school* and *meter*
(*schola, metrum*). Household terms like *ginger, millet,* and *radish* can
also be found in the same pew: the English word for *root* came from the
Latin *radix, radicis.*

But these two sources accounted for only a paucity of our Latin borrow-
ing; the biggie—70 percent of our language— came because of William the
Conqueror in 1066. Though proud of his status as King of England,
William was primarily the Duke of Normandy who had conquered

England as a means of enhancing his prestige at the French court—like a Dallas doctor buying a pasture out in Poteet or Pecos. He spoke only French as did his successor upon successor.

To further insure French as the language of the English nobility, the "English" kings also made a point of consistently importing their brides from high up in the French nobility. Shakespeare students will recall how Henry V courted the French princess (Renee Asherton), and how their son, Henry VI, selected Margaret of Anjou as his queen.

In fact, the people in England today would have to parlez-vous in French had it not been for a few minor skirmishes around Crecy and Poitier between the French and English armies. Historians called it a war. And as it began to drag on—toward its hundredth year—the resentment toward France grew so intense that the English actually decided to speak English. They tried! They tried! But with such a weak English vocabulary, they frequently had to substitute words from their native French. And since French is a Latin language, several thousands, yes, thousands upon thousands of words of Latin origin now tickle our tongue.

Soldiers, clerics, and monarchs all played a role in the Latin transfusion into the stream of English. The result is that our language is all the richer.

Q: In Sweden, students begin the study of language very early, which pleased me because languages were my favorite academic subject. English especially fascinated me: so many of the words looked like Swedish words. The English hound *looked like the Swedish* hund *(it was also* hund *in German); the English* cat *was related to the Swedish* katt *and the German* katze.

One way that English differed from Swedish was the accent. In Swedish the accent was always on the first syllable (same as in German), but in English it shifts. You have famous, *then* infamous, compare, *then* comparable, *and four different accents with* photograph, photography, photographic, *and* photogravure.

Is there any reason for this?

I'm interested in this not only because of my study of languages; I plan to remain in the United States and become a citizen. My children also are interested in languages.

Ingemar Johansson
Lighthouse Point, FL

A: Congratulations on your decision to become a U.S. citizen, Champ. Glad to have you aboard.

But getting to your question: the reason for the similarity of words in English, German and Swedish is that all three languages belong to the Germanic branch of the Indo-European family tree. Dogs even bark the same in all three languages.

You mention that Swedish and German words have a fixed accent on the first syllable. It's the same in English—with native words. But the words you mention are foreign words: *photograph* comes from the Greek; *compare* and *famous* from Latin. Historians tell us that this trait of the Germanic languages developed in the fourth century: the first syllable is always stressed unless the word is a prepositional compound. Examples of the latter are the English word *forget* and the German *vergessen*. This trait is so strongly entrenched in our language that if the accent (as with a foreign word) is not on the first syllable, it will try to get there, as it did with *infamous* and *comparable.*

If you dig back into your Latin and Greek, Ingemar, you will recall that the accent for the word *love* shifts from Latin *a'mo* to *ama'mus* in the present tense, and the Greek word for *foot* shifts from *pos* to *pod-os'* in nominative to possessive. In English the stress is fixed. It's only those foreign imports that give us trouble.

Frequently a word from another country enriches our language and we welcome it as heartily as we welcome a citizen from another country—especially one who is rich and a former heavyweight champion of the world with a handsome face that looks like no one ever laid a glove on it.

Q: As a student of useless knowledge, I've always been fascinated by trivia about English kings, especially anything that has to do with Richard the Lionhearted or Arthur of the Round Table.

Now today in class my history teacher said that King Richard spoke very poor English and Arthur never spoke a word of English in his life. What are the facts? Also, why was a seat at the Round Table such a great prize to some of the knights?

Ken Bethea
Tyler, TX

A: Your teacher is correct.

The best English that Richard spoke came when Anthony Hopkins played the role in *The Lion in Winter.*

During his lifetime, Richard spoke French as did all the "English" kings from William the Conqueror to Henry the Fifth, 1066 to 1399.

(The King's English also suffered under George I and George II, who spoke mostly German.)

But the broken English of King Richard was worthy of a Pulitzer Prize when compared to that of King Arthur, who probably never spoke a word of English in his life because, many scholars say, he probably never existed.

In the Middle Ages, the two most popular subjects for literary romance were Charlemagne of France and King Arthur of England. One was a historical character in his own right; the other a fabrication of Geoffrey of Monmouth. While interest in the historical character waned, popularity of the fictitious one skyrocketed right up to Tennyson in the Victorian Era and continues today via radio, TV, movies and even comic strips.

As with J.R. Ewing and his *Dallas* coterie there was something inherent in Camelot's clouds of glory that stimulated the imagination to romp through a never-never land of make-believe.

The basis for King Arthur and the accreting legends was Artoris, a Roman legionnaire, who remained in England with his GI bride when the Emperor retrenched to the continent. Artoris never got higher than morning-report clerk or first sergeant in the Roman army, but Geoffrey elevated him to the kingship.

As to your second question, a place at the Round Table was prestigious because seating was limited to no more than 150.

Besides, the Round Table was widely known for its square meals.

Q: This question doesn't pertain to the English language, only to England. Sitting here in Cotton Center, Texas, I keep asking myself how the English people can put out so much money for the royal wedding and all that when their country has so many other financial problems and unemployment.

Shari Carr
Cotton Center, TX

A: The question exceeds the length of our leash. So we submitted it to Gordon Rosen, a prominent London financier, who gave us the following answer.

"Just on economic grounds alone, we can defend it. What was the last American film that cost 20 million pounds and didn't run more than a fortnight? I believe it was *Heaven's Gate.* But here was something that had a live audience of one million and a TV audience of 700 million and didn't cost the British taxpayer a thrupence. The Queen paid for everything; the money had already been set aside in the royal exchequer for this occasion. And it wasn't that much money. We didn't have to build any elaborate sets; St. Paul's was already there, the soldiers already had their uniforms, and the bloody horses were in the stable. In fact, this generated money. Lots of it. This was sound economics.

"But we're talking of something more than economics, and it's hard for Americans to understand it because they have nothing comparable: in fact, very few nations do, unless it would be the Italians and the euphoria they feel at the election of a new pope. It's continuity, stability, vicarious identification, and roots. Here was something that went back to 1066, and you knew that you were a part of it. And you saw so many people who felt the same way as you did.

"Once in America I noted something similar during the Super Bowl hysteria. But even in the Super Bowl, someone had to lose. Here we were all winners and even had intimations of immortality."

You may get a slightly different version from the future King of England—should he ever visit Cotton Center—but at least you have the viewpoint of a London businessman.

Q: I was invited to Houston last year in my official capacity, and though I found the people hospitable and the language comprehensible—very similar to ours—there were three lexical items that I never mastered: huh *and* uh-uh *and* uh-huh. *What do linguists call this sound and how do they explain the difference among the three?*

If it is not impolitic, may I also inquire why the Americans, who have enriched our language with so many colorful words, would prefer these non-words, these grunts, to real words when our language has so many beautiful words to express meanings or emotion?

I guess I still consider it "our" language.

Sir Ronald Gardner-Thorpe
Lord Mayor of London

A: All of these are conversation markers, according to linguists, letting the speaker know that we are listening and following the message. The sound is a schwa, sometimes accompanied by a glottal stop. The difference between these three lexical items proceeds from intonation pattern and stress.

In *huh?* ("What did you say?") the intonation rises.

In *uh-uh* ("No") the stress is on the first syllable (iambic) and the intonation descends.

The opposite is true of *uh-huh* ("Yes" or "I understand" or "Keep talking") where the stress is on the second syllable (trochaic) and the intonation ascends. If the spelling doesn't begin with an *h,* there is a glottal stop.

The reason why Americans say *huh?* and the British emit *pardon?* probably proceeds from our preference for the informal and your predilection for the formal and refined. A Victorian literary critic, Dr. Richard Fulkerson, once pointed out that when an American grunts *huh?,* he is blaming the lack of communication on the party of the second part while in the British *pardon?* the speaker is accepting the culpability for the breakdown. Dr. Fulkerson was quick, however, to concede that this cultural-difference theory is pure conjecture.

One item that is not conjecture is the date of the first recorded observation of the presence of *huh* in the United States. Back in 1839, a European traveler recorded the following: "There are two syllables— *um, huh*—which are very generally used by the Americans as a sort of reply, intimating that they are attentive, and that the party may proceed with the narrative, but inflection and intonation are made to express dissent or assent, surprise, disdain. I myself found them very convenient at times . . ."

This European traveler, like yourself, was English. He also resembled you in another instance. Captain Frederick Marryat had had a distinguished military career.

Q: Your column should be of great value to me as a language teacher. There are questions that arise which seem difficult to answer. In all my years of teaching English and German, I have yet to find a good reason for gender classification in certain languages. Is there truly no rhyme nor reason? Does the science of linguistics shed any light on this question?

Ms. Connie Hudspeth
Lindsay, TX

A: Since scholars have never seen a language develop, they haven't a shred of evidence on the origin of grammatical gender.

Ignorance of facts, however, has never kept eager scholars from speculating. According to one theory, for example, man has an innate urge to classify (witness the work of current labels like *extrovert* and *introvert* or *liberal* and *conservative*). That theory maintains that the primitive German classified nouns by perceiving the forces around him: masculine, feminine, and neuter.

Sometimes this grammatical gender was natural gender—generally not. Thus a Fraeulein (Fräulein) was neuter and did not become grammatically feminine, a Fräu, until she married. Logic played no role in this categorizing.

Day, war, and *state* were masculine; *night, love,* and *world* were feminine. Was *world* feminine because the primitive Germans realized it was a woman's world? The oracle is silent. But you can tell your students that the language was made before the grammar.

It may also interest your students to know that our English language once had grammatical gender. *Wife,* for example, was neuter back in Anglo-Saxon times.

When nouns lost their inflection in the direct object and indirect object during the Middle English period, they also lost their grammatical gender—a break for us.

Today English is the only major language in the Indo-European family tree with natural and not grammatical gender.

True, ships are given feminine gender, as are automobiles ("Fill 'er up"), but this is attributive gender and has nothing to do with sex.

How well a student of foreign language masters grammatical genders depends considerably on the visual imagery with which he is endowed and the teacher with which he is inflicted. Study habits and tenacity of purpose always help.

Rewards are exceedingly great. "He who knows a foreign language," commented Ben Franklin, "is worth two men."

Intangible advantages accrue to the student of foreign language: insights into the beauty and structure of our own language, greater ease in composition and the chance to discuss sex on the most academic of levels—grammatical gender.

Q: This letter concerns the recent cutting off of funds for bilingual education. When will the conservatives learn that a problem will not go away just because you decide to forget about it? Wasn't it Aristotle who said "the direction in which education starts a man will determine his future life"?

Sixto Martinez
Houston, TX

A: The quotation you cite is from Plato, although Aristotle did echo the same sentiment a few years later.

As to the thrust of your letter, we have had considerable mail on this topic; some from liberals criticizing the current administration for cutting the funds, some from conservatives criticizing the previous administration for trying to solve a problem by "throwing money at it."

Frank Hodges writes: "Some guys made a bloomin' fortune by fighting poverty." Frank is from Irving, Texas.

Eleanor Galbreath of Sherman, Texas supplies us with a quote from Dr. John Finley: "I wish every immigrant could know that Lincoln spent only one year in school under the tutelage of five different teachers and he still was able to write the *Gettysburg Address.*"

The schooling of Lincoln's successor, Andrew Johnson, was even more limited: he never had a day of schooling in his life, according to Trey Snider, whose hobby is collecting trivia on the American presidents. The Plano, Texas student continues: "Other presidents who never went to college were Truman, Cleveland, Fillmore, Taylor, Van Buren, Jackson, and Washington. Never having been exposed to Latin, President Fillmore turned down an honorary degree from Oxford because no man should accept a degree he could not read."

This reluctance to accept a diploma one could not read was not shared by millions of Americans, according to Dr. Dennis Harp, trivia buff from Lubbock, Texas. "Do you know that 25,000,000 Americans are functionally illiterate, and a large percentage of them have a high-school diploma?"

The absence of academic trappings did not prevent Kemmons Wilson from building his own motel and then adding a couple thousand more Holiday Inns, according to Jerry Jobe, Dallas manager. "And do you know what? He never finished high school." Neither did Bobby Fischer, the great champion in chess, according to Dennis Cardinal O'Quane, himself no tyro in the manipulation of castles and kings.

A letter from Wes Jones, Dallas student of political science, informs us that an immigrant with a name like Karl Schurz could become Secretary of Interior without the benefit of a bilingual program back in the days of Lincoln.

Our readers seem to be telling us that life is a do-it-yourself project, especially in the mastery of a language.

Aristotle would agree.

* * *

Additional information came from a Dallas director of plays, Don Shook ("Noel Coward never finished grammar school; Orson Welles had only a total of three years") and Alba, Texas historian Patsy Gaby

("Benjamin Franklin had two years of schooling and Thomas Edison only three months").

Q: When I was studying in Germany last year, the question I heard most frequently from other language students concerned the reason for our extensive English vocabulary and its variety. They could not understand why sometimes I would refer to my car as "my buggy," while other times I'd say "my wheels," or "my heavy metal." Why does English have so many synonyms in this instance? All they say is "mein Auto."

Lynn Handley
College Station, TX

A: Language is a function of society, and whatever is important to that society will be reflected by a large number of synonyms. Thus the Eskimos have more than a dozen words for *snow* but no word for *coconut,* while in Samoa there is no word for *snow* but eight distinct words to describe the maturation of a coconut. The ancient Arabs had hundreds of words to describe *sword,* while the modern inhabitants of Trastevere (a slum near Rome) have a great number to describe the male genitals. "And 1,999 of them are vulgar," according to Isaac Asimov.

Because of the vital role that the automobile plays in American life, it was but natural that a large number of synonyms would develop (*rod, boat, vehicle, jalopy, clunker, limousine*) and that new ones would continue to emerge as the *driving machine* of Chrysler or the *mark of excellence* by Lincoln.

Sociologists also contend—since language reflects the things that occupy us most—that we may judge the intimacy of a relationship by the number of nicknames, pet names, or even profane names that we coin for a thing, place, or—person!

* * *

Dr. Norbert Elliot reminds us that we overlooked the word *car* and is kind enough to give us its fascinating etymological history. "*Car* was a moribund word in English until modern technology brought it back to life. By the middle of the nineteenth century *car* was only a poetic synonym for chariot, to which it is related. With the advent of the railroad, *car* gained a new lease on life by being used in the United States for what the English call a 'railway carriage.' ". . . but *car* really came to life after the term *motorcar* was adopted late in the nineteenth century for the automobile. *Motorcar* was shortened to *car,* which lost all its archaic and poetic associations in the brave new era of gas-guzzling machines." (*Word Mysteries and Histories.*)

Q: *We hear quite a lot these days about Black English with the trend appearing to be that Black English has earned a degree of legitimacy simply by virtue of widespread use among the black race.*

I contend that English is either properly or improperly spoken, according to its rules and laws of structure, and that it does not come in hues of red, pink, green, black, or purple.

Ralph C. McClure
Dallas, TX

A: There are two points of view at question: the linguistic and the social.

Ever since Babel, humanity has been debating the relative superiority of one language over another. During the Middle Ages, Latin was enshrined as infallible: after all, it was the language of the holy Church, the vernacular of the scholastic philosophers, the lingua franca of the universities. But by the 18th century, thinkers like Voltaire began to speculate that perhaps the language that contained the greatest amount of great works might possibly be the nonpareil of languages. Today, no language is considered superior, no dialect inferior, because each language is capable of expressing an infinite number of ideas through an infinite number of sentences. According to linguists, even dialects have their own distinctive grammar, a grammar that is both complex and logical.

Despite their ivory-tower isolation, linguists are also aware of the world of reality; in every country, one particular dialect has managed to dominate—the King's English in London, the Parisian dialect in France, standard American English of the United States. This is the language spoken by commentators, political leaders, and members of the upper socioeconomic class. In the United States, it is the one adopted by the actors on soap operas and in movies.

For obvious reasons, the melting pot we call the United States has fewer dialects than does the confusing caldron of our European cousins: our nation is younger; the population more mobile; and the influences of radio and TV are more prevalent. But we do have dialects, and one of these dialects is Black English which differs from standard English in both grammar ("he be" for "he is") and in phonology ("hep" for "help"). When philologists tell us that Black English is equal to standard English they mean that it is a system of communication complete and satisfactory for those who use it. But they are speaking about the language linguistically and not socially.

In some situations, Black English is more acceptable than, say, hillbilly English or Brooklynese. In other situations, however, that is not the case. The basic fact is that the most accurate indicator of one's social status is not the clothes one wears nor the vehicle one drives but the patterns of one's speech.

It has always been that way—ever since Babel and the Bible. ". . . thy speech doth betray thee."

III.

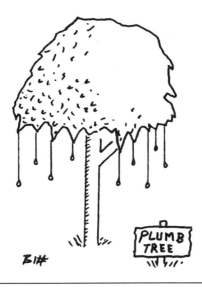

Regional English

Q: While visiting in Texas, I was a little puzzled to hear heavyweight George Foreman say he was going to "carry" his mother to Marshall. Now I know that George is strong enough to carry his mother from Houston to Marshall—or even Minnesota. But then I heard other Texans use "carry" in the same sense, and they were not as big as George. At the time, these Texans were also "fixing" to leave. In New York, "fix" means to make stationary or permanent and back in Cleveland it had another meaning. But none of these fine Texans had this "fix" in mind when they were "fixing" to leave. Is the Sun Belt ahead of the rest of the United States in coining new words?

Don King
New York, NY

A: In this case, Texas isn't ahead but just a little reluctant to give up some idioms that were once popular in England and in parts of the U.S. "Carry" in the meaning of "to conduct, escort, lead a person without reference to mode of travel" was used by Dr. Samuel Johnson in 1758, when he spoke of a lady carrying her horse for a thousand miles.

It had been used in this meaning previously in Samuel Pepys' *Diary* and in the 1611 translation of the *Bible* in a book well known to you, the *Book of Kings.*

Its first recorded use in the United States was in 1622: " We carried Indians . . . to the place where they had left their bowes and arrowes." Our dictionary, however, labels his meaning "dialectal."

Regarding "fix," in the meaning "to get ready for or determine to do or be something," it was first used in the U.S. in 1716 and gained a foothold in England, where it grew obsolete, in 1788. It is now considered "colloquial" in the U.S. Its last citation in the *Dictionary of American English* was in 1914: "I met schoolgirls . . . so painted up that they look as if they was fixin' . . . to be bad." One wonders how the expression could grow obsolete. The quotation was from *The Perch of Devils.*

On a more personal note, if you're *fixin'* to promote another heavyweight title match, we hope you'll select Dallas. We'll gladly *carry* you and the contestants to Big D.

Q: While traveling in Texas recently (the Dallas area), I overheard the following conversation: "I was proud to get out of that accident alive; I liked to got killed." I also heard a woman say she was proud she found a new apartment in Garland. Would you translate these for a traveling man who hopes to return to Texas?

James F. Sanderbeck
Arlington Heights, IL

A: Although suicide is the sincerest form of self-criticism in the other 49 states, people in Texas don't like to get killed. "Like" in the sense of "almost" is non-standard English, but it is quite common in Texas and occasionally used in the South Atlantic states. Its origin is uncertain.

"Proud" in the sense of "pleased, glad, elated" is not of Texas origin, although it is frequently used here, and can be traced back to Somersetshire in England, where it is still popular. Research reveals that "proud" was once used to describe certain mammals (mares and elephants), "in a state of sexual excitement, in heat." In 1727, some cupid wrote: "Make broth thereof and give her some twice or thrice and she will infallibly grow proud." The recipe? Sorry. We plan to bottle it and sell it.

One might guess that such use of "proud" may have given origin to the term "a pride of lions."

In any case, lexicographers classify the uses you mention as sectionalism and non-standard.

They rank alongside such expressions as: "He had his leg broken."

Only a confirmed masochist would "have" his leg broken.

Imagine a confirmed masochist seeking out a confirmed sadist to request: "Please break my leg."

Imagine the delight of the confirmed sadist in replying: "No."

Q: I have a question for Dr. McNamee. Many Yankees smile when we say "you all," but they say "youse guys." Which, if either, is correct?

Carol Richards
Dallas, TX

A: Both phenomena developed because of a weakness in the English language. Many years ago, the singular form was "thou" and the plural was "you." This pattern continues today in German, Spanish, and French in which distinct pronouns exist for the singular and plural.

But in English the word "thou" dropped from use and "you" became both singular and plural. Dropping into use was "youse," recorded as early as 1810 in Ohio. "You all" showed up in Virginia as early as 1824 (picked up from slaves). Both terms are attempts to overcome the loss of "thou." H.L. Mencken noted that the literature on the subject of "you all" is filled with bitterness.

Interestingly, while "you all" was considered colloquial and "youse" was considered downright illiterate in the second edition of Webster's New International Dictionary, the third edition merely defines the terms without comment.

Q: Can "y'all" ever be used as a singular? The Deskbook of Idioms and Idiomatic Phrases *published back in the 1920s says no, as does an article in the* Georgia Review *around 1960.*

In your column you once mentioned that y'all *developed (as did* youse) *because it was difficult for the word* you *to function as both singular and plural, especially after* thou *dropped out of the language. Recently, however, I've noticed how some young people are using "y'all" as a singular. Has anyone done any recent research on this subject?*

Michael A. Figures
State Senator
Mobile, AL

A: Your observation is correct. "Y'all" is sometimes used as a singular by some young people, and according to the Professor who researched the subject, it produces a certain distinctive flavor. In 1975, a Yankee professor, Nancy Spencer, did some research down south on this subject and reported her findings in *The American Speech*. "A salesgirl in the local store approached me with 'Can I show you something?' and when I had found some items, she said, 'Did y'all find something to try on?' And as I went into the dressing room, she added, 'My name's Debbie if y'all want any help with those things.'"

With this and other examples, the researcher concluded that "for some speakers, 'y'all' denotes informal social dialogue of a friendly nature. I have found it usually in questions and with verbs like *hope, think, want.*"

Her research also involved young adults among whom "y'all" seemed to indicate "group cohesiveness."

Political leaders often seem to have an uncanny ability to sense the public's sentiment and changes in speech patterns. You are a very discerning senator. We'd like to find out sometime how middle-aged Southerners feel about "y'all," especially those born in the South.

* * *

We did not have long to wait. Our discussion of "y'all" as a singular produced an avalanche of reprimands from Southerners: professional, semi-professional, good old boys, irate D.A.R.s, ex-service personnel, etc. One of the more printable letters made the following point: "The only guy I ever heard use "y'all" as a singular was a lady from upstate New York trying to act like a Southerner." As H.L. Mencken observed: "The literature on this subject is filled with bitterness."

The most illuminating letter came from one of the penitent perpetrators of the problem. According to this Alabama girl, during WW2 the service personnel from the South would frequently use "y'all" as a singular in front of non-Southerners to tease and deceive. But it was always with tongue-in-cheek. "I just can't imagine a real Southerner doing that except to tease—or to make a sale. Maybe we overdid it, but I see the deception is still going on—enough to deceive that there professor who was doing research on "y'all.'"

Q: Why do people in the southern states speak slower than northerners do?
Conrad T. Strugala
Irving, TX

A: The myth that Southerners talk slower because the warm climate slows down activity is exploded when you consider that as you approach the equator, Spanish, Portuguese, and other languages are spoken at a faster clip than Southern English. The hot climate theory would have made Charo outdrawl any Texan or Georgian. Anyone who has heard her trills and bursts of Spanish on T.V. knows her Latin tongue flies like a hummingbird.

Some scientific studies have shown that Southerners actually speak faster than Yankees—that is, they make more sounds per second. But while the Southerner is saying "cow's milk" with a drawled out "caeouwuz mii-iulku," the Yankee has moved on to other words.

Southerners take longer to say their words and sentences because their parents did and the parents before them. Perhaps some scholar who unlocks secrets in the history of the English language will one day identify which particular generation started the drawling process characteristic of the South.

Q: When I moved to Mississippi, I made every effort to be both conventional and inconspicuous. With the intellectuals, I would discuss idears; *on Sunday I would go to* choich *with the bourgeois; and down at the feedstore, I would close each parting with* "Y'all come back, hear?"

Best of all in history class I was suitably sympathetic with the South. But there I met my Waterloo, or should I say "Appomattox"? The professor accused me of prejudice because I referred to the "Civil War." I've already dropped the class, but what was I supposed to call the war from 1861–1865?

John Mark McKenzie
Starkville, MS

A: There's a constitutional implication here. Many historians prefer to call it "the War Between the States" or even "the War of Northern Agression."

You must remember, John Mark, that some professional Southerners still hoard their Confederate dollars in the dream that the South will rise again.

Pat Craig Coker of Texarkana, Texas saves both Confederate dollars and Dixie cups.

But never apologize for this kind of prejudice.

It's the greatest labor-saving device since the cotton gin. It enables one to form opinions without digging for the facts.

Q: Is it correct to use fur *as a substitute for* far? *For example, take the sentence "Its a* fur *piece from Bonham to Bug Tussle." Also, is there a difference between* further *and* farther?

Julie Thomas
Bonham, TX

A: Back in old Anglo-Saxon times, *farther* and *further* were different words *(ferther* and *furthor)* with different meanings; today they are increasingly interchangeable. In the future one of them will disappear from the language.

As of the present, *farther* can be used only when speaking of distances; *further* expresses some aspect of reasoning but also distance ("We have *farther* to travel but also some *further* details to discuss"). But *farther* is being used less and less, and according to some experts, will eventually be cut down by the scythe of Old Further Time.

Fur piece in the sentence you cite is a delightful bit of regionalism, but it is just that—regionalism.

Q: We featured some Valley Girls on our program. Since that time we have had several inquiries about Valley-Girl language. Has there been any study of this subject by scholars, linguists, or psychologists?
Leeza Gibbons
PM Magazine, WFAA-TV
Dallas, TX

A: There has been some study and it has revealed three popular misconceptions. To begin with, the Valley Girl is not confined to the San Fernando Valley. This ubiquitous miss is also indigenous to the Red River Valley, the Rio Grande Valley, Valley View Mall, in fact any mall in the United States, especially a mall in an affluent area.

The second misconception is that the Valley Girl is a mirror image of the flapper, who (threescore and more years ago) danced the Charleston, the bobby-soxer, who swooned for the crooners, or the hippy miss who just did her own thing. "Kiss my tuna," the Valley Girl would answer. "I am much, much younger than any girl of those groups." The life span of a Val is four years, between ages 13 and 17.

The third fallacy (and this one is shared by Valley Girls) is that their language is unprecedented, unfathomable, and revolutionary. Actually, Valspeak fits into a syndrome, the syndrome of secret languages; and though speakers of this secret language aren't aware, Valspeak is as closely governed by rules as are the classical languages of Greek and Latin. As examples will demonstrate, every word in Valspeak has been formed in a conventional manner.

CLIPPING: Part of the word is sheared away and the remainder comes to stand for the whole word (*Jell* for Jell-O-head, *coaster* for one who lives on the coast.)

COMPOUNDING: Two words are joined together to form a new concept. (*Vidbo* for *video* and *bozo,* a bozo who's been spaced out by video games.) Compounding is as old as the English language, as old as our Germanic heritage, e.g. *Kindergarten.*

FUNCTIONAL SHIFT: The ability of a word to shift from one part of speech to another (*blitzed, lensed,* and *amped* are three past participles derived from nouns).

ETYMOLOGICAL REVERSALS: A *vicious dude* is a good-looking boy; *outrageous, wicked,* and *insane* all mean "good" to Valley Girls.

ONOMATOPOEIC NEOLOGISMS: The sound gives echo to the sense (*Rolf* and *barf* mean to vomit; *scarf out*, to overeat; *gnarling*, disgusting, *geek*, an obnoxious guy).

Valspeak does differ from standard English in two instances: its use of conversational markers and its intonation. Only in Valspeak can an entire sentence be formed from "Y'know, like, OK, totally." Only in Valspeak can "Omigod" be stretched to encompass all 12 half-steps of the diatonic scale.

How do psychologists explain Valism? It is "another way of allaying adolescent insecurities," and without using the word *freeloader*, the psychologist adds, "This insecurity is deepened when the girl does not earn her own money but is dependent on her mother's credit card."

Q: I've been in Texas now for a fortnight and find your language very similar to the one we speak in England—except for your expression "where am I at?" Is this indigenous to Texas?

Mrs. James (Patty) Goode
Maidstone, Kent, England

A: This substandard expression is classified as an "intensive" in that it stresses the query about the location. Today it is heard mostly in the West and South and very much in the Southwest. But it has been traced back to 1859 and as early as 1903 appeared in what was once considered "the newspaperman's newspaper," the old *New York Sun:* "The business world wants rest; it wants to know where it is at." (Even in those days, analysts loved expressions like "the message of the market is murky.")

Though our Texan "where am I at?" may be confusing to you Britons, when we go to England we too are confused by the Cockney "where is my 'at?"

And you should be advised that Texans consider it an invitation to bad luck to leave your 'at on a bed. It's a cowboy superstition.

A pair of strange boots under the bed can also cause trouble.

Q: Down in deep East Texas where peaches are pretty and plums are dingy, we have an expression "plum pretty." Why don't we select a fruit that is both indigenous to the region and aesthetically pleasing?

Mary Jackson
Quitman, TX

A: The expression "plumb pretty" (note the letter *b*) did not germinate in the orchard but in the carpenter's shop and the surveyor's kit. *Plumbum* is the Latin word for *lead,* and a plumb line is a string with a lead ball at the bottom to help the surveyor determine perfect verticality. Anything that is perfectly beautiful then is plumb beautiful. Grammarians label this as an *intensive.*

Q: On my first visit to northeast Texas, I was surprised when people spoke about "arsh potatoes." On subsequent visits I learned they were talking about "Irish potatoes." I always thought potatoes came to us from Scotland. Anyhow, why this unusual pronunciation?

Grady Defoore
Houston, TX

A: The word *potato* comes from the Haitian word *batata* by way of the Spanish *patata.* Spanish explorers introduced the tuber to Europe from the New World. It was reintroduced in New Hampshire (1719) by immigrants from Ireland. Scotland had nothing to do with its popularity. In fact, the potato was once banned by the Presbyterian Church of Scotland because it is not mentioned in the Bible.

If the people of Quitman, Texas, are not *tarred* of hearing this, we would point out that one of the charming characteristics of the East Texas dialect is the tendency to pronounce an *i* as an *a* as in "the hard hand hit the boss with a tar tool and an arsh potato."

Q: In one of your columns you made a reference to the origin of the term "pork barrel." I have a different perspective about the origin of this as being symbolic of reward and incentive.

In my own oral (black) tradition, the story is told that the master of slaves surreptitiously placed barrels of pork on selected slaves' cabin porches. The tradition holds that this was a reward for "good work" and an incentive to continue other activities which facilitated the smooth operation of the plantation (including elimination or castigation of miscreants). One element of the modern (again, black) interpretation is that the status of the receiver of the pork barrel was enhanced because she or he could deliver favors at will to fellow slave-community members as a result of the fortuitous designation by the powers that be (or were).

I have found no reference to this in written material which I can cite, but as I mentioned to you, the story is well known and common among a number of black Americans across the country. I believe that my grandfather (the first free-born black in my family) repeated this to me as a story told by his father. Incidentally, could you tell me the roots of the expression "good old boy"?

Dr. C.W. Leftwich
Cleveland, OH

A: We are grateful for your observation and are happy to inform you that this oral tradition is confirmed in William Safire's *Political Dictionary:*

"The phrase probably is derived from the pre-Civil War practice of periodically distributing salt pork to the slaves from huge barrels."

In the *National Municipal Review* of 1919, C.C. Maxey stated, "Oftentime the eagerness of the slaves would result in a rush upon the pork barrel, in which each would strive to grab as much as possible for himself. Members of Congress, in the stampede to get their local appropriation items into the omnibus river and harbor bills, behaved so much like Negro slaves rushing the pork barrel that these bills were facetiously styled 'pork barrel' bills, and the system which originated them has thus become known as the pork-barrel system."

A story by E.E. Hale called *The Children of the Public* that appeared in *Frank Leslie's Illustrated Newspaper* also helped to popularize the epithet. The year was 1863.

We were unable to find the roots of "good old boy" but did find some material on the "good old" part of the expression. *The Dictionary of Slang* defines it as a "term of address or reference, generally affectionate, occasionally derisive" and traces it to Albert Chevalier in *The Little Nipper* of 1892. Shakespeare frequently used "good old" in plays (*As You Like It* and *Much Ado,* for example).

"Good Old Boy" might make a good, new title for a country song someday—if it already hasn't been used.

* * *

This discussion of the origins of the term "good old boy" brought comments from readers.

Evelyn Songe Scott of Dallas writes:

"The Dallas Morning News some years ago (perhaps in a column by Frank Tolbert or Paul Crume) printed a definition indicating the difference between a 'good old boy' and a 'redneck.'

"1. A 'redneck' drives around in his pickup truck and throws beer cans out the window.

"2. A 'good old boy' drives around in his pickup truck and puts his beer cans in a litter bag."

B.N. McEwen of Richardson, Texas has a theory regarding the term's origin:

"Most likely, it has roots with English-speaking Scottish immigrants (some spoke Gaelic).

"In Scotland 'boy' has the same meaning as 'man' in America. In Scotland 'lad' is used where 'boy' is used here.

"The adjective 'old' in some cases has become misused on both sides of the Atlantic. As used in this case, it is a term of endearment. Originally, it came from 'ole' of Middle English, meaning 'dear.' Lazy tongues and evolution of the printed word now has 'old' representing both 'old' and 'ole.'

"Then, 'old boys' would be close friends, family or merely those of one's own kind. Naturally the term was expanded into 'good old boy,' meaning a local person of the same background, moral values and socio-economic status as the speaker or writer.

"It is used primarily in the Southeastern and Gulf states of the U.S., where, of course, the largest concentration of Americans of Scottish descent is found."

We can only add that, without doubt, they put their empty Scotch bottles into litter bags.

Q: What is the grammatical status of hisself? *I travel to Oklahoma a lot and hear* hisself *more than* himself, *especially around Durant. Is this some sort of regionalism that developed in Oklahoma?*

Gary Caplinger
Bonham, TX

A: Hisself has been around since the days of King Alfred and developed in the same way as did the reflexives *myself* and *yourself.* It has always enjoyed some currency. One grammarian in 1762 wanted to outlaw *himself* and established *hisself* as the only logical form. He lost! So it continued to be considered bad English. Today it is classified as "substandard," even in the suburbs of Durant.

Q: I have some kinfolk in Georgia who refer to themselves as crackers. *I never thought this was a complimentary term. Yet they use it.*

Thomas Lane
Honey Grove, TX

A: Here we have an example of a semantic change in which a lexical item undergoes a change in meaning. According to a source back in 1766, a *cracker* was a member of "a lawless set of rascals on the frontiers of Virginia, Maryland, the Carolinas, and Georgia, who frequently changed their place of abode."

By 1836, it had risen to mean a "southern backwoodsman," and by the end of the century a sympathetic son of the soil, a poor white, especially in Georgia. Today it can mean any resident of Georgia.

Another source tells us that the *cracker* appellation originated in Georgia and Florida: poor whites started their day with cracked corn and gravy. Their breakfast never changed; and they liked it so much they had breakfast three times a day.

Q: Our travels in Texas were always pleasant. Back in the days when gas was plentiful, we would just get a gallon or two at each station to give us an excuse to stop and listen to people talk. The rhythm of the language was so lyrical, so beautiful. But at this place near Tyler, Texas they asked my husband if he would help them "pound the preacher." I don't think they recognized Jack. They seemed like nice people—Baptist, I think. But I've often wondered about that expression.

Mrs. Jack Dempsey
New York, NY

A: It's a custom in some rural areas of Texas to honor each new preacher with a *pound party.* Each guest brings some provision, originally in a one pound package.

The custom isn't confined to Texas, in fact. For example, a 1931 issue of the Durant, Oklahoma, *Democrat* reports "Caney Pastor Pounded." We also encountered the term in 1947 in Gainsville, Florida, where "The Methodist Church members had a pounding for Reverend Leo King and his wife."

Research reveals this colorful bit of Americana can be traced back at least to 1877. It has yet to appear in the *Oxford English Dictionary,* however.

Q: Where did the term "Texas Leaguer" develop? Local legend has it that it started right here in Texarkana in a park where the infield was in Arkansas and the outfield in Texas. Anything out of reach of the infielders was a "Texas Leaguer." The year was 1929. Can you confirm this?

Leon J. Coker
Texarkana, TX

A: We hate to ruin a good story but our research indicates that the place was not Texarkana but Syracuse, New York, and not 1929 but 1889.

It seems that three rookies from Houston—Bill Joyce, Emmet Rogers, and Arthur Sunday—had just joined the Toledo club in the American Association for a game against Syracuse. While the other players were swinging for the fences (and hitting long fly balls), the Texas trio was content to slap soft bingles through the infield. The exasperated pitcher (the record books tell us his name was O'Brien) roared out in disgust: "All them bums from Texas can do is drop in them (deleted expletive) *Texas Leaguers.*"

His remark reached the press. Reporters seized on it. But it took a long time for the term *Texas Leaguer* to become accepted in every franchise. In some places, a ball that was too far out for the infielders and too far in for the outfielders was called a *drooper* (Western League), or a *looper* (American Association), or *Japanese liner* (Pacific Coast) or a *Sheeny Mike* (International League). Some fans of the old *Harold Teen* comic strip dubbed it a *Leaping Lena.*

Eventually all of the leagues accepted the appellation *Texas Leaguer,* all leagues but one—the Texas League, where they still call it the *plunker.*

IV.

Holidays

Q: In leap year, what is it that leaps—the extra day? Writing poetry is my hobby, but when I started one on leap year, I got confused. Maybe the origin of the expression will help.

Herschel Walker
Dallas, TX

A: Leap year is an idiom, and idioms cause confusion, but maybe the origin of the idiom will help you in your iambic.

We wouldn't have that extra day were it not for the dilatory habits of Mother Earth. Oblivious of the 365-day calendar designed by Caesar and Pope Gregory XIII, our planet requires an additional five hours, 48 minutes, and 12 seconds to complete her orbit. Three theories developed as to the origin of the resulting term *leap year.*

1) According to legend, women were permitted to *leap* into matrimony every fourth year. Even saints were susceptible. Legend has Saint Brigid tendering a *leap year* proposal to Saint Patrick, who could decline because the custom had no legal sanction in the Emerald Isle. But the custom became law in Scotland. After 1228, if an eligible maid popped the question, a hapless swain was subject to a stiff fine if he refused. A similar statute followed in France in 1300 and later in the Italian city state of Florence.

2) According to popular theory, and the one accepted by the *Britannica Dictionary:* " . . . the first of March is not simply pushed on one day . . . but *leaps* over one day additional."

3) According to students of etymology, it had nothing to do with mythology, matrimony, or the month of March but centered on a *leap* of the moon. Medieval astrologers computed a 19-year lunar cycle. To compensate for Mother Earth's refusal to conform, they simply deleted the last day of the last month of their cycle. They called their cycle *Saltus Lunae,* which translated as *Leap of the Moon.*

Our word *assault*—one you've professionally encountered—comes from *saltus.* Anyhow, our idiom *leap year* developed from the translation into English. In German, it's *shift year;* in Czech, the *overstepping year.* Both are idioms.

The word idiom comes from a Greek root that means *peculiar.* Other words from the same root are *idiosyncrasy, idiolect, idioblast,* and another one that escapes us.

Q: Every February I ask Virginia to be my valentine. Since this has been going on for 35 years, maybe I should know what I'm asking her. How long have people been sending out valentines?

Chester Fuller
Quinlan, TX

A: You are probably saying "Come live with me and be my love."

Just as each year in the United States the swallows come back to Capistrano on March 19 (St. Joseph's Day), so in England every year on February 14 (St. Valentine's Day) the birds would choose their respective mates.

Valentine customs are quite old. Shakespeare's Ophelia sings, "I'll be your Valentine," and two centuries earlier, Geoffrey Chaucer spoke specifically of the mating of the birds.

"For this was on St. Valentine's Day

"When every bird cometh to choose his mate."

Fifteen centuries before Chaucer, on the feast of the Lupercal (which occurred at this time of year), young Romans would draw names out of an urn to determine their true loves, at least for that year (or a night). As with Christmas and Easter, the Christian fathers merely baptized a pagan holiday when St. Valentine's Day was named.

The first commercial valentines came out in 1800; comic valentines in 1870. They were sometimes called *penny dreadfuls* because they cost only a penny and the designs often were dreadful.

But we suspect that the valentine you sent Virginia wasn't dreadful and that it cost you a pretty penny.

Our favorite story about Valentine's Day comes from Priscilla Davenport, who edits this column.

When she was in the third grade back in Moundridge, Kansas, the most popular boy in her class got an early jump on Valentine's Day. Five days before the big event he placed valentines on the desks of five girls. The next day, he placed valentines on the desks of only four girls. The tension became unbearable when, with three days remaining, he distributed valentines to only three girls. On the following day, he narrowed the field to two.

And on the big day?

Priscilla, of course.

Q: I'm trying to locate an article about Abraham Lincoln and baseball. According to this story, Lincoln was going to use baseball to help the country get back on its feet after the War Between the States. Where can I find this article?

Also, what was the name of the famous French doctor who said much of his success came when he taught his patients to think positively?

Pete Rose
Cincinnati, OH

A: The article about Lincoln is in the October 1974 issue of *Esquire*, "Where Have All the Heroes Gone?" by Roger Kahn. In the piece, Kahn discusses a radio broadcast by commentator Bill Stern.

"According to Stern, Abraham Lincoln did not die in silence. From his deathbed, Lincoln summoned a nearby general and said, 'Keep baseball going. The country needs it.' The general's name, Stern cried out exuberantly, was Abner Doubleday."

It's an interesting episode except for one thing. It didn't happen. Stern fabricated it for his broadcast. But it was the age of the hero, and Stern apparently thought he had to pander to the hero worship of the day. He regularly made up two or three stories a week just before his broadcast. In one anecdote, he told of a boxing bout between a Notre Dame football star by the name of Knute Rockne and a West Point cadet called Eisenhower (it never happened) and of a meeting between Frankie Frisch of the Gashouse Gang and Pope Pius XII (it never happened). And that's the 3–0 count for tonight.

As to the medical doctor, at the turn of the century, Dr. Emile Coue taught his patients to begin each morning with "Every day and in every way I'm getting better and better." Or *"Tous les jours, a tous points de vue, je vais de mieurs en mieus."* (There must be something to Coue's notion because yesterday, for example, we couldn't even speak French.)

Some consider Coue the father of positive thinking. We're glad to hear about your interest in this subject, Pete, but we don't think you need any help in this direction.

Q: Since we're about to mark George Washington's birthday, could you tell us why the story about him cutting down the cherry tree became so popular? Also the one about him throwing a silver dollar across the Potomac. Are these stories authentic?

Ed Nagle
Fort Worth, TX

A: The cherry tree episode goes back to Parson Mason Weems, one of Washington's first biographers. His *Life of Washington* appeared just two months after the death of the president, but the cherry-tree episode was not even alluded to. Eight years later, "I cannot tell a lie, I did it with my little hatchet" makes its appearance in the *sixth* edition!

Despite the shakiness of Parson Weems' credentials—as a pastor he received his ordination papers via a mail-order catalog; as a writer he never let the facts get in the way of a good story—many reputable historians went along with the incident of the cherry tree.

You see, Ed, if there had never been an incident like this one, our infant republic would have had to fabricate one. Man has always yearned for heroes to help him transcend the daily disappointments and limitations of life. And so when the republic of manifest destiny appeared, it needed not only a hero but one of impeccable integrity. The cherry tree episode not only symbolized that integrity, it encapsulated it.

As to the silver dollar incident we suspect it is authentic. Geographers tell us that the Potomac was relatively narrow at some places; the local economist also relates, "money went much further in them days."

According to historian Harry Wade, one fact about Washington's biography that is never questioned is the length of his inauguration address—133 words. It's the shortest on record. Maybe it was because there was nothing he could criticize about the previous administration.

Q: Where does the term Mardi Gras *come from? Why does the celebration take place at a different time each year, and above all, where can we go to watch it besides New Orleans?*

Dr. Roy Renfro
Denison, TX

A: Mardi Gras is a public holiday not only in New Orleans but throughout Louisiana, Alabama and Florida. You could visit the carnival celebration in any of the South American countries or in the European countries that inherited Catholic culture: Italy, Spain, France or Austria, for example.

In these dark, inflationary times, however, we suggest you restrict your travels to Liberal, Kansas, where you could take part in the annual pancake race in which the winner will receive a prayer book from a preacher and a kiss from a British diplomat. Even less expensive would be a pancake supper at your local Episcopal church. True, not as colorful as the New Orleans celebration, but it does commemorate Mardi Gras.

Mardi Gras fluctuates because it is tied to Easter, a moveable feast that occurs on the first Sunday after the first full moon after March 21. The penitential season of Lent begins on Ash Wednesday, 40 days before

Easter, and Mardi Gras the Tuesday before Ash Wednesday. Got it? But you cannot count the Sundays.

Literally, Mardi Gras means *Fat Tuesday* in French; since fasting began the next day it was customary to consume all meat and fat in sight on that day. The Italian equivalent was carnival which meant *farewell to flesh*. In Germany they call it *Fastnachtkuchen* (fast-night cakes), and in England, Pancake Day.

Shrove Tuesday, the other appellation in England, was derived from the medieval practice of confessing one's sins on this particular Tuesday in preparation for Lent. Otherworldliness, the theme song of the Middle Ages, rang loud and clear during this penitential season. The verb *to shrive* meant to confess and receive absolution, an aesthetic experience akin to the catharsis of drama. The three-day period of Sunday, Monday, and Tuesday was known as *Shrovetide.*

The pomp and pageantry of the carnival season has attracted thousands of scholars, but two items still need to be thoroughly researched: the early beginnings of carnival, and the reason why the popes curtailed it to three days (it used to begin on January 6.)

As to its origin, medievalist Miroslav Hanak traces it back to the Saturnalia of the Romans and eventually back to the spring rites in prehistoric times. Concerning its curtailment, pop historian Jill Bardwell theorizes that the pre-Lenten period was defeating the purpose of Lent: "Too many of the laity were neglecting penitence; too many of the clergy were neglecting the *Bible;* and too many of both were showing up in *Booze Who.* "

Q: Why is Julius Caesar *taught in high school? The longer I teach, the more I realize that this play is too complicated for students at the intermediary level. I myself am not sure whether Caesar is the hero, or Brutus. Maybe you could answer this question before the Ides of March.*

Nancy Jones
Irving, TX

A: Julius Caesar became part of the high school curriculum way back when Latin was a required subject. Administrators thought it would be an excellent companion piece to add to the enrichment of *Caesar's Gallic Wars,* especially since the forensics department had already incorporated "Friends, Romans, countrymen . . ." into its exercises. In addition, the PTA liked plays devoid of dirty lines. But, as you noted, it is not a simple play. The fundamental problems of sympathy (who is the hero?) has divided the critics, the directors, and the public into separate camps.

According to the critics, it is Brutus' play. Their chief argument is structure. Shakespeare's usual pattern is to introduce early the tragic flaw of his protagonist; in this case it is the excessive idealism of Brutus. The conflict within Brutus culminates in the death of Caesar, which is also the high point in the fortunes of Brutus. Since the climax of a Shakespearean tragedy coincides with the high point in the fortunes of the protagonist, this plot fits the pyramid perfectly. Also in a Shakespearean tragedy, the protagonist makes one mistake at the counterstroke which brings about catastrophe: Brutus gives Antony permission to speak at the funeral and the conspiracy is doomed; so is Brutus. There is also a catharsis when we hear the line, " . . . This was the most noble Roman of them all."

On paper, it is Brutus' play.

But not in performance, argue the directors. Although Caesar speaks fewer than 150 lines, has but four opportunities to elicit sympathy in the first half of the play, and only a ghost of a chance in the second, it works better on the stage when Caesar is played as the sympathetic character. Robert Glenn, director of the Dallas Shakespeare Festival, even affirms that Shakespeare intended Caesar as a Christ figure.

During intermission of the play you get a third point of view from the public: "I think both of them guys, Brutus and Caesar, both are heroes," (Mickie Johnson, Denison, Texas carpenter); "My sympathies fluctuated," (Bill Brousseau, Dallas wildcatter); "There are two heroes with one systolic rhythm," (Janet Lawhon, Dallas newscaster). And so the debate continues. The public thinks there are two heroes.

The next time administrators select a Shakespeare play for high school students, they should consider *Richard the Third*. It's a much simpler play, and students could relate it to the agonies of the Ewing family. After all, little Richard was probably the prototype for J.R.

Q: As a nurse in a polyglot hospital, I've noticed that a baby addresses its mother with "mama" not only if it is an English-speaking mother, but also if she is Chinese. With Thai and Vietnamese, it is also a similar sound. Why is this? Is it the same with other languages too?

Elizabeth Germaine
Medical City
Dallas, TX

A: It's also *mama* in Romanian, *matka* in Polish, *motina* in Lithuanian. In fact, the word for *mother* starts with the letter *m* in all the Latin, the

Germanic, the Balto-Slavic languages, and then some: *madre* in Spanish, *moder* in Swedish, *mitera* in Greek, *mema* in Estonian.

It would make nice writing to say that there is some mystical reason for this phenomenon, but actually it is basically physical. The baby is exploring the limits of its vocal apparatus and comes up with the consonant *m* and the open vowel *a*. The *m* is a labial consonant, as far forward in the mouth as the kid can go, while the *a* is formed deep in the mouth.

This theory also explains *anya* (the Hungarian word for mother) *aiti* (Finnish) and *nana* (Albanian). Even though the consonants are not labial, they are close to it on the alveolar ridge (in the front of the mouth) and the vowels are open and in the back of the mouth.

Students of linguistics have also pointed out that the names for other caretakers who meet the child early in life also follow this pattern. The English *nanny* and the German *Oma* are examples.

* * *

A music major informs us that the first song children sing also follows this pattern: *na-na; na-na*. The letter *a* is formed deep in the throat; *n,* on the alveolar ridge. Why children sing this ditty in just about all the countries in the world independent of any other influence no one seems to know—anymore than why they always sing it in minor thirds.

Q: Your column once demonstrated how the word for mother *began with the letter* m *not only in English but in a lot of other languages, too. Since this feature appeared on Mother's Day, we're sort of asking for equal time on Father's Day. This question is really from my father: why does the word for* father *begin with the letter* f *in English but with the letter* p *in so many other languages? Is there a reason for this?*

Sean Maguire
Telephone, TX

A: There's not only a reason, there's actually a law, a very Grimm Law. Back in the 19th century while researching linguistics in the Black Forest, Professor Jakob Grimm discovered that if a word started with a *p* sound in Latin, its German counterpart would begin with an *f* sound (and English is one of the Germanic languages).

From *pater* to *father* is just one of the examples. In French, it is *pere* and in Spanish it is *padre*. But there are other examples: from *pe* comes *foot*, *piscis*—*fish*, *penna*—*feather*, *primus*—*first*, *plenus*—*full*. It developed systematically.

After the research, Jakob Grimm (and his brother Wilhelm) then enunciated Grimm's Law: the original voiceless stops of *p, t, k(c)* of Indo-European languages (preserved today in Latin) were changed to *f, th,* and *h* in Germanic languages. Latin *tres* became *three* in English; Latin *centum* became *hundred, caput—head, canis—hound,* etc.

It was while researching the language patterns among the peasants in the Black Forest that the Grimm brothers came across some fascinating and earthy anecdotes. And the world is richer today because of the publication of *Grimm's Fairy Tales.*

Q: Would you do a column on the word Halloween *and some of the practices that go with it such as the witches and the grotesque costumes that go with trick or treat?*

Mark Spencer
Sulphur Springs, TX

A: 'Twas the night before Christmas, and they called it *Christmas Eve.* By a similar linguistic process, the night of October 31, the eve of All Hallows (All Saints Day) became *Hallowe'en* or *Halloween.*

During the Middle Ages, each saint was honored with a special day (St. Patrick's Day, St. Crispin's Day, etc.) but when the population of Heaven exceeded 365 the medieval church instituted All Saints Day to honor those saints not mentioned on the calendar. In other words, everyone in Heaven was honored on November 1.

Originally, November 1 had been New Year's Day among the ancient Celts, a time when (as in many cultures) the dead flocked back to mingle with the living. When this belief persisted after the coming of Christianity, church leaders shrewdly moved All Saints Day to November 1 (it had previously been celebrated in May) and set up All Souls Day on November 2 as a special day to pray for the souls in Purgatory (the Catholic version of scholastic probation). It was around this time that the eve of All Hallows became known as the time favored by witches and sorcerers.

It was also around this time that hospitality committees began preparing banquets to honor the visiting ghosts. At the end of the feast, masked villagers, representing the souls of the departed, would parade to the outskirts of town leading the spirits away—a practice that is reflected today when children dress up in grotesque costumes and beg for candy or fruit. So much for the treat.

As for the trick, it too goes back to pre-Christian times: the mischief could always be attributed to a hobgoblin on the haunt.

And so on Halloween night kids will come to your door every witch
way.

*Q: Approximately where and when did the expression "poor as Job's
turkey" originate? Job was a character in the* Bible *and the turkey was
indigenous to America. Second, all of a sudden the word* eclectic *appears
to be quite popular and you see it more and more in the press. Any special
reasons?*

                                                      Rhome Tyree
                                                      Kilgore, TX

A: Since writers are constantly warned to avoid cliches like the plague,
they are ever on the lookout for fresh similes and metaphors.

Back in the 19th century, Sam Slick (penname of Thomas C. Hallibur-
ton)—seeking a metaphor for utter destitution—invoked a barnyard muse
who inspired in Slick the notion of a turkey so poor that he had only one
feather in his tail.

Eschewing the cliché "poor as a churchmouse," Slick turned to the
Bible and found Job.

The sufferings of Job descended on his turkey—and stuck.

How poor was Job's turkey?

Well, as Slick had it, that turkey was so poor he had to lean against the
fence to gobble.

Moving to your second question, we should note that although *eclectic*
is derived from the Greek word meaning *selecting,* eclecticism wasn't a
characteristic of Greek philosophy. It was the successors to the Greeks,
the Romans, who were the great eclectics, notably Cicero whose philosophy was about a third Platonism, a third Stoicism, and another third
everything else.

It is axiological that a period of great creative activity is followed by a
period of eclecticism, as the situation in the United States now gives evidence. The great contributions today are by the research team, the bibliog-
rapher, the explicator, the commentator, and especially by the specialist in
information retrieval. This is one reason for the popularity of the word
eclectic. Eclecticism is the philosophy of the day.

But there are other reasons.

Time was when individual credos and kingdoms competed with each
other, each claiming that it alone possessed the truth or maintained a
pipeline to God. Only a dwindling number of institutions make that
claim today.

Another characteristic of our time—perhaps one for which it will be remembered—is the speed with which we accept a new idea and then reject it. As a result of these tendencies, eclecticism has become a way of life and the word has achieved greater currency.

Eclecticism isn't confined to ivory towers, of course.

Eclectic cooks do it. Decorators do it. Re-decorators do a lot of it. A Porter named Cole did it. And so did Sam Slick.

Q: Who wrote the first Christmas carol and why are some of them so much better than others?

Mike Coker
Texarkana, TX

A: The father of the Christmas carol is St. Francis of Assisi, who brought music out of the church and into the festivals of the streets, out of the Latin and into the native tongue of the populace. The distinctive flavor of his carols was their human warmth; he believed that you could be pious and jolly at the same time.

The year that he brought forth the first Christmas carol, 1223, he introduced another world-shaking innovation: in Greccio, Italy, he set up the first manger scene with a real babe and live animals. Again there was tender emphasis on the humanity of Christ. Within a few years, Christmas, which had been a reverence for a disembodied spirit, now became an earthly feast of massive popular participation with manger scenes in every church in Europe. It was easy for peasants to identify with the poverty of Christ, and now they could sing Christmas carols even though they did not know Latin. By the sixteenth century, thousands of carols had developed from the work of sophisticated musicians; others just grew the way that folk songs have always grown, being passed along from one generation to the other by word of mouth.

Any authorship that has been verified is generally traced back to a clergyman. *Silent Night* was the work of an Austrian priest; *Hark, the Herald Angels Sing,* by Samuel Wesley; *Joy to the World,* by Isaac Watts. Not so today. *White Christmas,* the most popular Christmas song of the 20th century, was written by Irving Berlin, a Jewish immigrant. *What You Gonna Call Your Pretty Little Baby?* came out of the ghetto, where blacks could identify with the couple who found no room at the inn.

Francis of Assisi did not compose *Jingle Bell Rock,* but he would have approved of its full-throated gladness. He also would have appreciated *I'll Be Home for Christmas* and *I Saw Mommy Kissing Santa Claus* and other Yule ditties that celebrate man's yearning for community and affection.

Why some carols are better than others is for music critics to decide. But we can hint at the distinctive flavor of the Christmas carol itself. The secret of the popularity of Christmas—even before it was commercialized—is that it combines the here and the hereafter, the human and the divine.

Never noted for regular attendance at Sunday school, Voltaire once conceded that man is hungry for spirituality: "If there were no God, we would have to invent one." A later writer added, "Christmas gives us an opportunity to follow the birth of Christ and his re-birth in us, wherever that relationship takes us."

But Christmas also celebrates man, especially his search for family and companionship.

And the beauty of the Christmas carol is that it expresses in song both of these urges—the quest for divinity and the endless mystery of human love.

Long before Friedrich Nietzsche wrote it, Francis of Assisi lived it: "Without music, life would be a mistake."

Q: How long has the mistletoe been identified with Christmas? Also how long has the custom of "under the mistletoe" been associated with this particular holiday?

Virginia Carol
Bonham, TX

A: Yes, Virginia, there is a mistletoe legend that has been around a long time—even before there was a Christmas according to the Roman historians. One of them, Pliny the Elder, reported that this magical plant was thought by some to induce fertility, cure ulcers, banish spirits, and protect hearth and home against thunder.

Two thousand years later, we are still touched by the reverence with which Pliny describes the treatment of the plant: "On the sixth day of the moon . . . Druid clad in a white robe climbs the tree and with a golden sickle cuts the mistletoe which is caught in a white cloth."

It was because of the reverence associated with this plant that it became the plant of peace: enemies who chanced to meet under the mistletoe would not fight but would lay down their arms and declare a truce for that day.

So if enemies would declare a truce because of the mistletoe overhead, the routine for dreamers and lovers is easy to conjecture.

The hanging of mistletoe at Christmas and New Year's was one of the many pagan customs carried over into the Christian era; in this case without any symbolic justification (as in the case of the egg at Easter, the evergreen at Christmas), but simply as a charming custom.

As to the exact time when kissing under the mistletoe started, historians have been unable to pinpoint it.

But there is one other point about mistletoe that Pliny noted that raps imperatively today for dreamers and lovers.

It is POISON!

Q: I'm looking for a book that deals with the mysterious birth of folkheroes. I mean no irreverence by this question, but isn't it true that much of the mystique of Christmas proceeds from the virgin birth of Christ?

C. Ling Silvia
Aberdeen, MD

A: Wherever there are heroes, there are stories of mysterious births or periods of concealment. Moses was hidden in the bulrushes; Buddha had been a white elephant before he was conceived; John the Baptist was born of a barren woman; the Blackfoot Kyotis, of a clot of blood; Adonis, of a tree that wept spicy gum for its fruit. At the time of Isaac's conception, Abraham was 100 years old and Sarah was past 90.

Where this motif first entered, we do not know, except that it showed up with the Germans (Siegfried), the Egyptians (Isis), Africans (Lituolene), and the Persians (Zoroaster). Neither do we know why this is a necessary ingredient in the folk-hero cult, although there is one theory: Ever since the fall of Adam (or his equivalent), mankind has been yearning for a new beginning, for a Messiah. This Messiah cannot be touched by human frailty: the Aztec Quetzalcoatl was born of a virgin: Buddha's birth was "unsmeared by impurity."

There are many books on this subject, but two of the most popular are Joseph Campbell's *Hero With a Thousand Faces* and Otto Rank's *Myth of the Birth of the Hero,* although the latter gives a slightly Freudian slant to the motif.

As to your other question, the virgin birth is only part of the mystique of Christmas. There is also the charisma of the Christchild and the transcendence that is evoked by a mission of love. And since the Yuletide giving of gifts and sharing of dreams that takes place at this time seems to proceed from a love born in Bethlehem, we have a mystique that is difficult to duplicate and—unless you see Christmas through the eyes of a child— impossible to explain!

V.

Grammar, syntax, and sin

Q: In my English elective, the prof keeps telling us to write "in parallel." Being a P.E. major, I know what parallel bars are, but I don't think that's what he's talking about. Also, being a country boy, and sort of big for my size, I hate to ask dumb questions. But what does he mean?

G.L. Martin
Mount Vernon, TX

A: What he is talking about is parallel structure, the use of similar grammatical structure for similar ideas. Compound subjects, compound verbs, compound sentences, and the like are all examples of parallel structure.

Awkward: "Gene is good (adjective) at tennis; an expert dancer (noun), and mixes (verb) well."

Correct: "Gene is a star tennis player, an expert dancer, and a fine mixer."

The main purpose of parallel structure is clarity. It guides the reader to a neat, clear relationship of ideas: "Government of the people, by the people, for the people . . ."

Many famous passages gained their renown not so much by their content as by the conciseness of the parallel structure:

"as Caesar loved me, I weep for him;
"as he was fortunate, I rejoiced at it;
"as he was valiant, I honor him, but as he was ambitious, I slew him."

Sometimes parallel structure will develop in conversation. When the late Bennett Cerf was reviewing the work of novelist Pat Webb, the publisher reportedly told Webb: "You have a great future as a novelist. You weave the plot admirably; you develop the characters superbly; and—you have a filthy mind."

Since this repartee took place along Greenville Avenue in Dallas, we had a unique situation: parallel structure along parallel bars.

Q: If most can be used as an adjective and almost as an adverb, then is "Most everyone left" grammatically correct? Everyone, a pronoun, is the word modified, so to use almost would have an adverb modifying a pronoun. Yet "Almost everyone left" is what is heard. To use most agrees with the grammar rules, but it sounds incorrect.

Donna Korman
Arlington, TX

A: Your question brings up three interesting points. First, *most* is an informal contraction of *almost*. To the ear of the purist, "Most everyone left" sounds incorrect, but there is no theoretical or grammatical reason why *almost* cannot be contracted into *most*—on an informal level. You hear it frequently today, especially in the speech of young people.

The second is that *almost,* though we think of it as an adverb, can also function as an adjective, as in "Most everyone left," the sentence you cite. Coleridge, Thackeray and Hawthorne all used *most* in this fashion and the usage is approved today by the *Oxford English Dictionary* and the *Britannica World Dictionary.*

What you are saying—and this is the third point—is that "part of speech" is as much a function of use as it is a static descriptive term. This functional shift is one of the beauties of English. It also offers a cornucopia of possibilities for writers of the sort who tragically relate the story of the butcher who backed into the grinder and got a little behind in his work.

Q: With Angelo Dundee as my trainer, it's natural that I should pick up a bit of Ali's boxing style. But I'm curious about some of his speech patterns. Is "float like a butterfly, sting like a bee" grammatically correct? When I finish boxing, I'm planning on becoming either an entertainer or a teacher. Now's the time to start working on my image—and my grammar.

Sugar Ray Leonard
Palmer Park, MD

A: You are using "like" as a conjunction, and though the *Oxford English Dictionary* lists *like* as an adjective, adverb, noun, preposition and verb, it still doesn't approve of it as a conjunction. Certainly, it does fulfill the requirements of a conjunction: it joins two clauses. It is also becoming popular informally and eventually will be accepted formally, at least in the United States. But strong opposition remains.

Let's form a wall against advertising corruption of the language, argue the purists who feel the word has been foisted upon us by commercials.

Those with a classical background will generally go down the line with the purists, but it's difficult for us to understand so much antipathy: Edmund Spenser employed *like* as a conjunction in 1596, Shakespeare in 1608, Keats in the 19th century, and F. Scott Fitzgerald in the 20th. "Like as a father pitieth his children, so the Lord pitieth them that fear him" occurs in the Holy Bible.

What a one-two combination: Shakespeare and the Bible. What other authority could you want except Muhammad Ali—and you already have him.

We're glad you're thinking of teaching. You have much to offer. More-over, you'll encounter no discipline problems.

Q: Reference is made to your column in which you elucidated how the word damn *could serve as noun, verb, adjective, adverb, interjection—five parts of speech—but that* kiss *could function as six.*

Since I have been teaching English grammar for more years than I care to remember and have received more osculations than I care to admit, I'm just curious what these six parts of speech are.

Donna Saucier
Cumby, TX

A: Half a century ago Robert Ripley defined *kiss* in his *Believe It or Not* and then demonstrated how, according to definitions set down by gram-marians, the word could function as a noun, pronoun, conjuction, verb, adverb, and preposition—six parts of speech. It went something like this:
1. A noun because it is common or proper.
2. A pronoun because she stands for it.
3. A conjunction because it joins together.
4. A verb because it expresses action.
5. An adverb because it tells how much she loves him.
6. A preposition because it has an object.

Q: I seem to recall that the word loan *is a noun, and that* lend *is a verb. Nowadays I constantly hear* loan *used as a verb. What is the correct usage now? Are these words interchangeable?*

Mrs. C. Richard Gholston
Dallas, TX

A: Lend is a verb, and *loan* is both a verb and a noun except in England where it is only a noun. While in the States you frequently hear: "will you loan me five bucks until payday?" Such usage is condemned in Britain, especially in southern England, where it is labeled a "vulgar American-ism." It wasn't always so, however. *Loan* was used as a verb in England before the Pilgrims set sail from Plymouth.

As to your second question, the two words aren't interchangeable. *Lend* is never used as a noun. We never say, "Give me a lend." Also as a verb, *loan* is restricted to requests for money or something just as good. "If you won't loan me five bucks until payday, will you at least loan me your new car?" But in some instances we never use it that way. If Mark Antony had said, "Friends, Romans, countrymen, loan me your ears," he'd never have made it out of the New Hampshire primaries.

"Distance loans enchantment" sounds like a commercial for Hockshop John and lacks the lyrical quality of "distance lends enchantment."

Q: Now that liquor has been legalized even in Ladonia and gambling has spread beyond Vegas, I'm wondering about the social status of "ain't." It's permissible to use it now, ain't it?

Carlton Robardey
Ladonia, TX

A: Not the way you use it. It does occur in the speech of many cultivated persons in every part of the U.S., especially in the expression "ain't I?"— but not in the written form. One reason for its currency is that, though we have contractions for "is not" and "are not," the language supplies nothing for "am not."

Another reason is that (aside from "y'know") English has no equivalent for *no es verdad, n'est pas,* and *nicht wahr.* Thus "ain't" fills a lacuna and may win acceptance possibly in written and certainly in oral communication—someday. But that day isn't today. "Ain't" still bears a bit of a stigma, even among semi-literates, in its written form. As to its origin, the word and the controversy antedate Ladonia and Vegas and go back to Colonial days. It ain't something new.

Q: On TV, when the police read an arrested man his rights, they tell him that anything he says can and will be used against him in a court of law. Suppose the arrested person merely commented, "It's a nice day today." Why would that necessarily be used against him?

Confused in Forney
David L. Zimmerman
Forney, TX

A: In real life as distinct from "reel" life, the police officer never tells the arrested man that anything he says can and will be used against him, only that it *may.* We are paraphrasing a letter from Dallas Police Chief Billy Prince.

To quote him directly, ". . . I cannot say why a television script used the words *can* and *will* or why an actor portraying a police officer would utter these words. However, I can and will send you the information card Dallas police officers use to advise arrested persons of their Constitutional rights.

"You will notice that the card does not say *can* and *will* in reference to the use of statements made by arrested persons. Instead, it reads 'any statement you make *may* be used as evidence against you in court.' The word *may* denotes discretion on our part."

The top policeman further elucidates: "Therefore, to answer your reader's question, unless the arrested person's statement about the weather is directly related to wrongdoing, it would not be used in court."

Chief Prince also wishes our reader a nice day and "fine weather."

Q: Even before fallout, Three Mile Island and nuclear fission, we were warned about split infinitives. What are some of the hazards, the side effects and, above all, when is an infinitive split?

Ms. Joyce Hill
Madisonville, TX

A: An infinitive is split when an adverb comes between the word "to" and the infinitive, e.g. "to gradually realize." Split infinitives have a long history in our language. They've had a bum rap.

Many of our early grammarians outlawed the construction because the infinitive form of the Latin verb is never split. But they were forgetful that the Latin infinitive (*laudare*) cannot be split, that the best English writers always have been splitting infinitives, and that the number of verbs employing "to" with the infinitive has been increasing ever since Beowulf put a half nelson on Grendel (compared to the number of verbs that did not use "to" with an infinitive back in Anglo-Saxon days). Regrettably, the rule found its way into many of our prescriptive grammar books.

Stylists will tell you that many times a split infinitive is needed to avert ambiguity. In the sentence "The Pope's formula for making holy water is to really burn hell out of it," we would have a squinting modifier without the split infinitive. The meaning of the sentence shifts when written: "The Pope's formula for making holy water is really to burn hell out of it."

Sometimes a split infinitive helps to gain emphasis. "By constructing a square bathtub, the entrepreneur hoped to more than solve all ring-around-the-bathtub problems."

A shade of meaning can make a difference. But when too many adverbs intrude, the split infinitive becomes incorrect, just as any excess usually is incorrect.

If there must be a rule, it should be: split an infinitive whenever you feel like splitting one, but don't start enjoying it too much.

Q: Has snuck *sneaked into accepted usage as a past tense for the verb to* sneak? *Within one week I encountered this form of the verb in two novels* (The World According to Garp *and* The Second Son) *and in a story in* The Dallas Morning News.

Jacqueline O'Neill
Dallas, TX

A: At this moment, *snuck* is still admitted only on an informal level, a little like Dizzy Dean's "he *slud* into third base," generally jocosely.

Unlike Dean's linguistic aberration, which never got beyond third base, *snuck* will eventually sneak in, so popular has it become.

Q: Please comment on the following usage. "I dislike him *doing that." I know it should be "I dislike* his *doing that." But I don't know what grammatical rule governs it.*

H. Knox
Dallas, TX

A: The rule you are looking for is "A pronoun before a gerund is in the possessive case; a pronoun before a participle is in the objective case."

In the sentences you cite, you don't dislike *him* personally. The emphasis is not on the pronoun *him.* You dislike what he is doing. The emphasis is on the gerund *doing.* Therefore, we use the possessive case *his.*

But suppose that the emphasis is on a noun or a pronoun. It would then be incorrect to use the possessive case, for the verbal would no longer be a gerund but a participle. Examples will illustrate.

"We witnessed a joint session of Congress settling the marijuana issue."

(The emphasis is on *Congress; Congress* is in the objective case, and *settling* is a participle.)

"Congress' settling the issue is still up in smoke." (The emphasis here is on *settling; settling* is a gerund and *Congress* is in the possessive case.)

With pronouns, the dichotomy is even clearer.

"We caught *him* running away with the money." (Objective case with participle.)

"*His* running away with the pin money was a defeat for acupuncture." (Possessive case with gerund.)

Q: What is the difference between a gerund and a participle? They both look the same.

Michell Ballew
New Boston, TX

A: They look the same because they are the same. The difference comes from their function in the sentence. Note the following sentences.

"Covering all broad issues is the aim of the new feminist magazine." Or: "The new feminist magazine, covering all broad issues, was a howling success."

In the first sentence *covering* is a verb used as a noun and is a gerund. In the second, *covering* is a verb used as an adjective, and we have a participle. Sometimes the difference between a participle and a gerund can be clarified by repartee:

"Do you like bathing beauties?"

"Don't know. Never bathed any."

Q: Dallas citizens pay millions of dollars to teach children that an adverb should modify a verb. Then they pay another million to paint signs saying DRIVE SLOW. "Slowly" is the adverb.

> Alexa Karnes
> Breckenridge, TX

A: So is "slow." Back in the days of Beowulf, adverbs ended either in "lice" or "e." The "lice" ending eroded to "ly" (as in "quickly"), and the "e" dropped out completely. "Slowe" became "slow." And cars became faster.

Q: "Years ago while driving through Forest Park in Fort Worth, squirrels were seen in the trees." I tried to use this sentence in a theme, but my girlfriend changed it. She said it was a grammar error. It makes sense to me the way it is. There used to be a lot of squirrels there.

> Bruce Raben
> Ft. Worth, TX

A: It makes sense to most everyone, except to someone in the teaching profession (where your girlfriend may have an affinity). An English teacher would label your error "a dangling participle" because, as the sentence stands, the squirrels were driving through Forest Park. Incidentally, there are still a lot of squirrels there.

Q: Now that I've been out of the classroom for several years, I feel less sure of my grammar, especially the distinction between "good" and "well." Would you please clarify these for me?

> Senator John Tower
> Wichita Falls, TX

P.S. I just saw three grammar mistakes in an eight-word sentence: "The democrat party is gaining strength in Texas." Am I correct in maintaining that there are three grammatical mistakes here?

A: Concerning "good" and "well," the first rule involved is that an adjective modifies a noun ("Jack is a *good* singer.") and an adverb modifies a verb ("Jill also sings *well.*")

After verbs of sensing, however, *(feel, smell, taste, look)* we use the predicate adjective. The Steelers may smell *bad* this year, but they look *good* when they play the Cowboys. Winston tastes *good,* but you may prefer to sneak one of those English imports you carry in that "gold" cigarette case the journalists mention (unaware it's really brass). This is the second rule: the syntax calls for the predicate adjective after verbs of sensing.

It's true that "well" is frequently used as a predicate adjective. We feel *well* because we take our bran and yogurt whether we like it or not. *Well* here refers to a state in contradistinction to the use of "good" referring to bodily sensations. A woman we know felt *good* because she gave the old beggar a dollar for a cup of coffee. And her husband felt grateful.

Some grammarians try to justify the use of "badly" ("We felt *badly* about the unavoidable delay.") on the ground that the emphasis is on the verb, but most authorities consider this to be hypercorrect.

Now all of this concerns formal English. Your mechanic may tell you that your engine runs *good.* Rarely will he say that it runs *well.* He probably will say that it runs like hell. As you know, there's a difference between English that is written and spoken.

Concerning your postscript, we too found three errors. "Democrat" is a noun while this sentence calls for the adjective; "Democratic" should be capitalized and "Party" should be capitalized. With scrutiny, you may find other mistakes in this sentence—other than those of grammar. But sometimes it's *good* to leave *well* enough alone.

Q: I'm concerned about the verb that follows "ham and eggs." Sometimes a customer asks, "how are the ham and eggs?" Yet another customer, on the same day, will ask "is ham and eggs the best thing you got?" Now I know that the customer is always correct, but the manager should know the correct grammar when he brings the order.

Gene Street
Dallas, TX

A: What is at stake here isn't just ham and eggs but collective nouns, words that denote groups of things regarded as single units. If the unit is referred to, then a singular verb is correct; but if the individuals in the unit are in question, we need a plural verb.

Examples:

Singular—The number of inchworms is decreasing every year.

Plural—A number of inchworms are now studying the metric system.

Singular—The whole family was furious when we eloped, especially his wife.

Plural—The family, now resigned, have gone about their individual duties.

Singular—The laity is distinct from the clergy.

Plural—Since the ecumenical movement, the laity are now studying the members of the opposite sects.

Singular—The wages of sin is deductible as a business expense.

Plural—Wages are better in Dallas than in Dime Box.

Some collective nouns are nearly always used in the singular, e.g., "party" and "harem." The Party has several political jokes, and some of them may get elected. Long before Wall Street, the harem was known as a prophet-sharing institution.

Note how the word "none" is always used in the singular, and "trousers" in the plural.

Plural—Dancers have only ten good years before the bottom drops out.

Singular—None of the dancers was doing anything illegal, although one was putting a motion before the house.

Plural—Pleated trousers are ideal with a silk shirt or with a stuffed shirt.

We plan to drop over for some ham and eggs. Do you have any organically grown?

Q: Would you please settle an argument in our office concerning subject-verb agreement? Some people insist on using are *in the sentence, "There are approximately 10,000 square feet of competitive space in the market area." I thought a plural noun which shows weight, extent, or quantity is singular and takes a singular verb. If this is true, then* is *would be the proper verb.*

James Freeman
Dallas, TX

A: The verb choice reflects whether the speaker is thinking of a unit or of individual parts. Example: "The budget committee decided that 10,000 square feet *is* too much space for your office." Or: "More than 10,000 square feet *are* available throughout the building." With the sentence "There *is/are* approximately 10,000 square feet . . ." usage is divided.

Q: *Which is correct? "My name and address* is/are *John Doe, 1303 Pothole Street, Anytown, Texas."*
I know about the rule that when two subjects connected by and form a unit, the subject is regarded as singular and takes a singular verb. But how do you tell whether the two subjects form a unit?

S.L.
New Boston, TX

A: Again, the person thinking of the items as a unit will probably choose a singular, and the one thinking of the items as separate parts will probably choose a plural. The choice is up to the speaker.

Q: *Announcers always say "Sports* is *next." Would it not be more correct to say "Sports* are *next"?*

Clyde C. Childress
Dallas, TX

A: Reasonably, it would depend on how many individual sports are to be offered. If baseball is to be followed by bowling, boxing, and basketball, then *are* would be correct. But, generally, we think of sports in a collective sense and go along with "Sports *is* next."

Q: *About 68 years ago my college English teacher told us to never use the word* gotten, *saying it was passé. Have you ever heard of such a thing? I have been confused about it ever since.*
I recently read that the English have dropped the ten. *He told of an old-fashioned teacher who wouldn't give up the idea of using* gotten. *He went to another town on some business and wired his wife: Come over for show, have gotten tickets. The telegram read* got ten *tickets. His wife brought eight friends. That cured him.*

Mrs. Julian Free
Irving, TX

A: We have received a number of questions along this line. The verb *get* has got a problem—actually, two of them.
The first is that while other irregular verbs have three distinct forms in the infinitive, past and past perfect (*go, went, gone; see, saw, seen; take,*

took, taken), this verb offers an option for the past perfect. You can say either *get, got gotten* or *get, got, got.*

The second problem is that *gotten* hasn't been used in England for well over 200 years and its use by Americans impresses Englishmen as "rathah old fashioned and not to be expected in the speech of a people that prides itself on being up to date."

Aping the British, many genteel teachers have tried to stamp out *gotten* with the aphorism *gotten is rotten.* Nevertheless, it is still acceptable in the United States at least in the meaning of *acquire, receive* or *become* but not in the sense of *have.*

The language would be poorer without this choice of verbs. Try to think of substitutes for *ill-gotten gain, hastily gotten up program,* etc.

So, if you've got it, flaunt it.

Q: Have the rules of English grammar changed in the past three decades (since I was in school)? Ever more frequently I hear on radio and television programs and see in print the usage of I rather than me as a direct object. Example: "John asked you and I to go." Is me a dirty word?

Mrs. Frances Clark
Hugo, OK

A: The sentence "John asked you and I to go" is both puzzling and entertaining. Suppose you didn't go, would John ask I to go by I self?

The overuse of "I"—this incorrect use of "I"— seems to proceed from uncertainty. In every profession there's an uncertainty and a stopgap solution. When Mark Twain would lose his place during a lecture, he'd pound on the pulpit until his train of thought was restored. In moments of uncertainty, baseball pitchers throw a beanball and boxers circle to the left. Mechanics put in a new part and send a small bill; doctors take out an old part and send a big bill.

In the first grade, children learn that it's incorrect to say "Me and him went home together." The objective case is wrong in this instance. But somewhere between the first grade and graduate school something went awfully wrong, such as telling kids about their right to their own language. Yet they still remembered from their first grade days when the objective case could be incorrect in some instances. So in their uncertainty, they now not only avoid it, they abolish it, especially when "I" sounds so much more elegant. In linguistics, they label this a "hypercorrection."

Getting back to your question: no, the rules of grammar haven't changed. They are just not being studied as much as they once were. And unless there's a return to basics, we're in danger of losing our links to the giants of literature who used grammar correctly.

Q: Students ask my sister (who is a teacher of English), "is Ed Jones really six foot nine?" She answers, "No. He is six feet nine."

I have three questions on this matter. Is this still the only correct form: six feet nine. *Second, what about a* six-footer? *Third, what about a* six-foot pole?

Ed (Too Tall) Jones
Dallas, TX

A: All three of the examples you cite are correct: *six feet nine, six-footer,* and a *six-foot pole.*

One source of the confusion comes from a grammatical error in a song we all love to sing badly: *Five foot two, eyes of blue.* This is a technical mistake. However primly, it should be: *Five feet two, eyes of blue* . . . and we don't really like it that way.

But, another source of confusion is that a *pole six feet long* is the only correct form. And the final source of confusion was that previous grammarians were afraid to take a firm stand. But now, thank God, they can verify their position at the Vatican from a *six-foot* Pole who speaks five languages and who follows boxing in ten.

Q: I only *have one question to ask. Would it not be better to say "I have* only *one question?"*

I was taught in grammar school that "only" should immediately precede the noun it modifies.

Some journalists, TV, and radio announcers and sportswriters frequently put "only" before the verb.

I noticed this last season when an announcer, talking about the Dallas–Los Angeles football game stated that Staubach "only threw 15 passes."

One sportswriter, referring to the Pittsburgh running game, said the Cowboys "only allowed 66 yards."

Please advise which is the correct usage.

Edward Thomas
Dallas, TX

A: We have *only* two answers. The first is to quote the rule: ". . . the word *only* should be placed as close as possible to the word it modifies." The second is to tell you to ignore the rule.

When you say "I *only* ate two pancakes," from the stress and intonation it is clear that you had no intention of drinking them.

Written English is following this trend. "*I Only Have Eyes for You*" made it all the way from the bar and boudoir to the sheet music from Tin Pan Alley; whereas "I have eyes *only* for you" or "I have eyes for you *only*" sound as if they should be played on the comb. It's simply a matter of what is good idiom, and the human ear—which is half poet—is your best judge.

Other adverbs that fall into this syndrome include *almost, even, every, exactly, hardly, just, nearly, and,* and *scarcely.*

Some purists still insist that *only* be placed as close as possible to the word it modifies, and they do have a following, a respectable following.

But they are not the *only* ones who are correct.

Q: In the last year or so I have noticed a change in usage away from what I was taught in Miss Myra Brown's English Six at Woodrow Wilson High School 40 years ago: a sentence in which the subject is a plural followed by the copulative "is." I suppose that in the following example, from a definition of "strabismus" in a flyer from a society for the prevention of blindness, viz., "One or more muscles of the eye is out of balance . . ." the copywriter reasons "One . . . is" rather than ". . . muscles are." Then there also is the sentence beginning with "There is," and this phrase is followed by a plural. I think I've seen this in mail advertising letters but also in newspapers, magazines and technical writing.

Max L. Plaut
Dallas, TX

A: You may be giving the copywriter too much credit in assuming that the reasoning took place when the singular verb was chosen. Compound subjects joined by "or" or "nor" are tricky to match with verbs, but careful usage requires that the subject closer to the verb should determine the verb form.

The faulty use of "There is . . ." when a plural subject occurs later in the sentence can be found easily among writers and speakers who do not realize that in this context "There" is an expletive and never the subject. Thus, standard usage would require, "There is a fly in my soup," but "There are bats in his belfry." Because the subject of an English sentence is so often the first word, the positional force of "There" makes us want to use a singular verb before determining the number of the subject that occurs later in the sentence.

Q: A preposition is a bad word to end a sentence with. So, there. Could you give me a ruling on this and tell me where all this started?

Renee Witterstaetter
Texarkana, TX

A: First of all, there's nothing wrong in ending a sentence with a preposition. As to how it started, authorities say that it goes back to John Dryden, the poet and essayist. We've always suspected that Dryden may have made the comment with tongue in cheek and never dreamed what effect it would have on English teachers in, say, Corsicana or Sulphur Springs.

Q: When visitors come to our funeral parlor, I ask them "Who do you want to see?" Should I say "who" or "whom"?

Peters Funeral Home
Greenville, TX

A: It all depends on whether you want to be formal or informal. Both are correct. No matter how hard precisionists and pedants try to keep "whom" in the language, it is destined to go the way of the beer opener because the drift in our language is against it. The other relative pronouns ("which" and "that") also had a different form in the objective case and both of them dropped out early. It's only a matter of time. The bell will toll for "whom."

Q: With regard to your comments on the use of a preposition with which to end a sentence, I believe that the late Sir Winston Churchill had the following to say: "The use of a preposition to end a sentence is something up with which I shall not put!"
So there.

J.C. Taylor
Lancaster, TX

A: Your version of Sir Winston's statement differs from his words usually quoted as the punch line of a favorite story circulated among grammarians. It seems that during World War II, a young military officer was given the unlikely assignment of editing one of the prime minister's speeches. Remembering his schoolbook rules, he revised a sentence ending with the word "with." The statesman put the would-be editor in his place with the rebuttal: "This is the kind of pedantry up with which I will not put."

Closer examination of the quotation—if indeed Sir Winston uttered those words—shows that the story often used in response to those who object to ending a sentence with a preposition doesn't actually apply because in this sentence *put up with* is a verb unit, and *with* isn't a preposition at all.

In such questions as "What did you hit him with?" or "Which fork did you eat with?" the final *with* is clearly a preposition, and ultra-purists might avoid using it at the end of a sentence by revising the sentences as "With what did you hit him?" or "With which fork did you eat?"

The usual word order of the sentence you quote would be, of course, "something I shall not put up with," using "put up with" as a verb unit. Note the difference between "with" as a preposition in "What did you put the wallpaper up with?" and, as part of a verb unit, in "How much nagging did you put up with?"

A favorite grammatical riddle that confuses prepositions with other parts of speech requires a sentence that ends in five consecutive prepositions. The answer comes as a question a child asks after he sends a parent upstairs for a bedtime story and the parent returns with the wrong book. The child asks, "Why did they bring that book that I did not want read to out of down for?" The final word qualified as a preposition, but *to* is part of the verb unit; *down* might qualify as an elliptical preposition in some analyses. A less analytic parent would say, "Shut up and go to sleep."

Q: What is the pluperfect subjunctive? I think I get the humor of the following rejoinder, but what does the pluperfect subjunctive have to do with it?

Visitor from Boston: "I say there, where can I get scrod around here?"

Policeman: "Where are you from, Jack? I've heard the word a hundred times, but this is the first time in the pluperfect subjunctive."

J.A. Myrick
Madison, WI

A: The pluperfect is the same as the past perfect tense. We use it when a past action is complete before another past action takes place. "The dentist didn't hurt me as much as I had expected." Our expecting had taken place long before the dentist began to drill.

The subjunctive mood is used for relating conditions contrary to fact. "Now if I had had your money" . . . "if you had only known . . ." "if she had only kept quiet," are all examples of the pluperfect subjunctive.

The *Britannica Book of English Usage* explains mood:

"Mood is the most elusive feature of verbs; it refers to a writer's or speaker's attitude toward what he or she is saying. Verbs change mood to indicate whether one is speaking of factual matters (indicative mood); giving a command (imperative mood); or speaking of desired, conjectural, probable, or suggested matters (subjunctive mood). The optative mood, once taught in classical grammar, expressed hoping or wishing and is now included in the subjunctive."

All humor proceeds from incongruity. The incongruity here proceeds from the fact that the policeman is trying to make a verb out of a codfish, to place that verb in the pluperfect subjunctive, and he doesn't understand either. The best way to ruin a joke is to explain it.

SHE ACCEPTS ME... SHE EXCEPTS ME... SHE ACCEPTS ME...

VI.

Homonyms, synonyms, sin, and interlopers

Q: Is there any difference between imply *and* infer? *None of the dictionaries in our office discusses this topic.*

Nancy Wagner
Seagoville, TX

A: We infer from your question that you mean the difference on both the formal and informal levels.

Formally, the answer is yes. Informally, to the regret of many careful speakers, the answer is no.

In formal English, a writer *implies* while the reader *infers;* a speaker *implies* or insinuates while the listener *infers* or deduces.

Examples will clarify. "After reading the financial report to the press, the chief of the Korean CIA *implied* that he may have to lay off several American congressmen." The members of the press would then do the *inferring.*

On the informal level, *infer* is now used so frequently instead of *imply* that the important (to some ears) if delicate distinction between the two is fast disappearing from our language, except among the literati.

Current dictionaries list both *insinuate* and *suggest* as synonyms for *infer,* a concession to foggy thinking and to the fact that the word is undergoing a semantic change.

You may come to distrust office dictionaries. According to a recent survey, most office dictionaries are more than 20 years old.

Offices bloom with new calendars each new year. Dictionaries just get older.

Q: I'll appreciate any help you could give me with assume *and* presume.

I've always used the two words interchangeably but I'm not so sure now that this is correct. Usually I'm speaking in the past tense—referring to some misunderstanding—and I'll say: "I assumed *you meant . . ." or "I* presumed *you meant . . ."*

Someone mentioned the other day that presumed *was more correct. We went to the dictionary for help but really only got more confused.*

John Wheeler
Fairfield, TX

A: Both *assume* and *presume* contain the element "to take for granted," but *assume* is the milder of the two.

Assume means to suppose, to put forth a hypothesis, with or without basis for belief. "Let's assume the Rangers win the pennant, will you go with me to the World Series?"

Presume means to consider likely, to regard something as true because there is no evidence to the contrary. Thus in early October you could say: "Since the Rangers lead by five games and the other contenders are in a slump, I *presume* we will win the pennant."

Note also that while *assume* means to "take something for granted," *presume* often connotes "to take too much for granted." For example, "During the World Series I would not presume to walk into the Ranger dugout without proper credentials and a chew of tobacco. That would be presumptuous of me."

These words are troublesome. To confuse them is a low order of misdemeanor. And until you are convicted by a jury of your peers, your innocence is *presumed.*

Right, Dr. Livingstone?

Q: I would like to read your comments on current usage of convince *and* persuade. *I believe that* persuade *is passing into oblivion at the expense of* convince.

> Bill Payne
> Dallas, TX

Q: Has the phrase "convince him to do something" always been in use? I don't remember seeing and hearing it when I was in school many years ago.

> Pat Arrington
> Dallas, TX

A: The distinction between *persuade* and *convince* still holds. You persuade a person to do something; you convince him *of* a fact; or you convince him *that* such and such is a fact. But you never convince him *to . . .* This is unacceptable.

Basically, *persuade* implies argumentation that brings about a change of position so that action will result:

"His former broker persuaded him to buy Braniff stock."

But Braniffless Alexander Pope remained "convinced of the sweet reasonableness of the universe."

Q: I wrote you quite a while back to "try and get" some information for my son regarding the differences between "accept" and "except." I shall try once again, hoping for a response in your column.

> Mrs. Arthur L. Bergman
> Dallas, TX

A: We have tried to answer as many of the questions we receive as we possibly can—*except* yours. And we certainly *accept* the responsibility.

There's no problem when "except" is used as a preposition and "accept" as a verb as in the previous sentence. As a verb, "except" means just the opposite of "accept."

Until your son feels secure in differentiating between "accept" (to receive) and "except" (to exclude), he would be wise to circumvent the problem by substituting "make exception to" for "except."

Our apology for the delay in getting to your question and we reiterate our policy of "accepting" all questions and "excepting" none.

Q: My son in Boulder wrote recently asking for some clarification between the words "effect" and "affect." I answered as fully as possible, although he indicated that he had already studied these words in the dictionary. Perhaps other people would appreciate some precise explanations of the differences in both meaning and use between these two often-confused words.

If you print the answer, I shall send him a copy.

Jean A. Bergman
Dallas, TX

A: This question is one of those most frequently asked by students of English grammar, punctuation, and usage.

There are several reasons for the confusion. To begin with, despite the histrionics displayed by pedants while vocally emphasizing the difference between "AAAfect" and "EEEfect," they are pronounced the same, both with a schwa. To compound confusion, some lexicographers don't help much when they define "affect" by telling us it means "to have an effect on."

So let's try to simplify things.

A good working rule is that "effect" is a noun and "affect" a verb. Another helpful hint is that it is the same "E" in "effect" as in "rEsult" and both these nouns have the same meaning as evidenced by "cause and effect" or "a cathartic effect" of "a law of little effect." In most cases, that's all one needs to know about "effect." It's a noun and means "result."

Now, your son may sometimes encounter "effect" used as a verb in the formal meaning of "to produce a result." For example: "The citizens effected many reforms; the reforms affected the citizens." Or: "The 15 beers affected Jane's vision, but a quick trip to the sauna effected a speedy recovery."

At this point, it becomes obvious that the verb "affect" means "to influence." Does Marie Osmond affect you? Or Joan Blondell? (Depending on your age.) Or Robert Redford? (Depending on your gender.) Or Francis X. Bushman? (Depending on both.)

The other meaning of the verb "affect" is "to put on." For example: "The cowboy from Corsicana 'affected' an Oxford accent."

We hope this disquisition has brought about the desired effect.

We would have employed "affect" also in that sentence but that might smack of affectation.

There's always a catch, however.

In the interest of completeness, we should point out that psychologists like to use "affect" as a noun and that they accent the first syllable with a resulting distinct vowel sound. This is a highly specialized, esoteric use of the word. And, anyhow, no one expects psychologists to be conventional.

Q: Will you please comment on what I think is misuse of the words "sit" and "set." To me, a human or an animal "sits." But a human "sets" down an inanimate object or "sets" a plant on a table.

Miss R. Rubeck
Dallas, TX

A: We get many questions about the "sit-set" difficulties along with queries about "rise-raise" and "lie-lay."

A good working rule (it's an oversimplification, but a good working rule) is to line up "sit, rise, lie" as intransitives and "set, raise, lay" as transitives. For example, you "sit" down by yourself, but you need *something* to "set." You "rise" up by yourself, but you need *something* to "raise." You "lie" down, but you must have *something* to "lay." Grammatically, the transitive verbs require an object to complete their meaning.

The "lie-lay" combination is doubly deceptive because the past tense of "lie" is also "lay"—"lie, lay, lain."

For instance "I had just lain down" is the correct form. Granted, it's seldom heard. Only the most dedicated devotees of the English language seem to have clung to "lain."

Q: I was "raised" in Hunt County, so I thought. Now my mother tells me I was "reared" there. Which is correct?

Dr. John Weddle
Rockwall, TX

A: In this case, there's no reason to raise the issue. Both of you are correct. "Raise" occurs more frequently in both popular periodicals and parlance while "rear" is usually reserved for formal occasions. Your mother, however, is in good company. Shakespeare, Milton, and Tennyson used "rear" in the sense of "to foster, nourish and educate." In the time of *Beowulf,* it was, in fact, the only correct form.

Long before Sony, Honda, and Volkswagen, we were swamped with imports. The Romans didn't spend all their time lying around eating grapes, they were too busy exporting words—roughly half the English vocabulary, in fact. But "raise" was smuggled in, from a different source: Scandinavia. The import ran parallel with the Anglo-Saxon "rear," and, in time, enjoyed greater currency than the other form and even developed meanings not expressed by "rear."

When visiting your mother, you can avert domestic discord by saying "brought up," a term widely accepted. And your grandmother would understand "fetched up"—if she ever lived in New England.

Q: For 50 years I have spent a number of hours each week setting to paper some of the great experiences I had as a hunter and fisherman in my youth. The correct usage of such words as "lie" and "lay" and "raise" bug me unmercifully at times. For example, in a story I just read the author said "he lay there for a long time." I would probably say 'he layed there for a long time' and be incorrect. Right?

I have another question. In preparing a manuscript to send to the publisher, should it be double spaced, with triple spacing between paragraphs? Also what is the proper indentation for the beginning of a new paragraph? Any help you can offer will be appreciated.

Ed J. Byrne
Dallas, TX

A: "Lie" is intransitive; "lay" is transitive which means that "lay" requires an object to complete its meaning. Think of the letter "n" in "intransitive" as meaning "no"—no object—and you will have no problem with "lie" and "lay" or "rise" and "raise" or "sit" and "set."

The confusion between "lie" and "lay," is doubly compounded since "lay" is the past tense of "lie." The three principal parts are "lie" and "lay" and "lain." For example: "He lay there for two hours." Or: "She had already lain down."

If it is any consolation to you, many great writers of the 19th century (Lord Byron, Wilkie Collins, and Anthony Trollope) consistently confused these two verbs. Why not disregard your phobia, and, taking the advice of Alexander Pope, write naturally as possible. If the content is good, editors will accept it and assign some unemployed Ph.D. to differentiate between "lie" and "lay."

The same holds true of spacing and indentation. Hit hard on content and, unless the publisher has special stipulations, let the form be such that pleases you. *Writers Magazine* gives a list of literary agents who claim to be willing to help beginning writers, but eventually it will be the content that sells. Back in 1951, *Harpers* magazine accepted "The True Believer" from an unknown, Eric Hoffer, single-spaced and—in longhand. It's said that Thomas Wolfe sometimes wrote on butcher paper. There is simply no substitute for quality. So if you have something to say, then say it. You may get a "rise" out of it. You may even get a "raise."

Q: During the negotiations for the hostages, former President Carter once excoriated the Ayatollah for flaunting *international law, when* flout *would have been the correct word choice. Why are* flaunt *and* flout *so frequently misused? Do they have a common origin linguistically?*

Tim Campbell
Mineral Wells, TX

A: Both words are not misused, only *flaunt,* as in the example you cite. The two words are confused not only because of phonetic similarity but also on account of emotional connotation because both suggest defiance. *Flaunt* means to make a defiant display; *flout* to mock or scoff defiantly.

Etymologically, there is no connection. *Flaunt* is related to the Old Norse word that means "to run back and forth," while *flout's* ancestry is a Middle English word that means "to play the flute," subsequently, "to whistle at," and eventually "to mock at," as we know it today.

There is still a distinction between these two words, and pedants will remind us that we *flaunt* our ignorance when we *flout* this distinction.

But once you've got it, why not *flaunt* it?

Q: My honors class in English would appreciate it if you would do a column on the already—all ready *syndrome. Specifically, would you point out A) is it correct to use* all ready *to refer to a singular antecedent; B) is it correct to use* already *as an interjection to express impatience as in "all right already"?*

Theresa Johnson
Sunnyvale, TX

A: Let's start with the fundamentals. *Already* is an adverb and means "before the time specified," e.g., "The team was *already* on the field." *All ready* is an adjective phrase and means "completely prepared," e.g., "They were *all ready* for the kickoff."

When demonstrating the use of *all ready,* grammarians generally select sentences that revolve around a plural antecedent ("We were *all ready* to eat."), but the singular use is equally correct ("She is *all ready* for bed." Or: "She is *already* in bed.").

The use of *already* to express impatience ("all right *already*") is dialectal and for the present unacceptable in formal circles. Since it is commonly used by New Yorkers of Jewish extraction, philologists have traced it to the Yiddish (and German) *schon* which sometimes means "already," sometimes is untranslatable. What New Yorkers mean by "all right already" is best left untranslated.

Q: Please include the distinction between eager *and* anxious *in your column. May you enjoy the holiday season.*

Ruth Lane
Nacogdoches, TX

A: The distinction between *eager* and *anxious* started early. They come from two different Latin roots, and careful writers who try to preserve that distinction use *anxious* when doubt or worry exists and eager when the mood is one of joyous anticipation ("She was anxious when the flight was two hours late for she was eager to get started"). The anxious are fearful; the eager beaver is hopeful.

Note the derivation. *Anxious* comes from the Latin word for choking *(angere),* while *eager* is derived from *acer,* which meant sharp or pungent. Shakespeare's Horatio spoke of "a nipping and eager air" on a cold night in Denmark.

Despite this cleancut distinction, in recent years we have frequently heard *anxious* used in place of *eager* ("Jeffry Ann was anxious to visit her wealthy uncle"). Although purists protest this promiscuity, such a usage has a certain psychological justification in that all eagerness contains a modicum of uncertainty.

On the other hand, *eager* is never used in place of *anxious.* We are all anxious when we get a letter from the Mafia or KGB but no one is ever eager to receive one.

Q: *What is the difference between* fewer *and* less, *if any?*
Karin Campbell
Dallas, TX

A: *Fewer* is used for countable items: "There are fewer apples in that basket . . . There are *fewer* people dying of bubonic plague . . ."
Less is generally employed to express quantities, items in bulk, or abstractions: "Scholars are learning more and more about less and less and eventually should know everything about nothing."
Regrettably, fewer and fewer writers are observing this nicety, and the distinction is becoming less and less. The distinction, however, does exist; and first-rate writers observe it, as do most speakers.

Q: *In our accounting office, we often refer to the "principal" in preparing a balance sheet. We further mention a "principle." Can you provide us with a sure-fire, easy-to-remember recipe for "principal" and "principle"?*
Mary V. Egan
First National Bank
Dallas, TX

A: This is a three-part answer. We'll do the easy parts first.
Principle gives us no trouble. It is always a noun and means *fixed rule* or *axiom* ("the *principles* of geometry never change"), a *fundamental truth* ("according to the axiological *principle,* things are essentially right"), or *a rule of conduct* ("Hector was a man of high *principles;* everything he stole he gave to his mother").
Principal as an adjective poses no problem in spelling if we remember that it fits into the pattern of *historic-al, music-al, politic-al* adjectives that end in *al.* As the examples demonstrate, it means *first, foremost,* and *chief.* "Hortencia's *principal* ambition was to become a plastic surgeon. The *principal* factor in her decision was an economic *principle*—that patients can be made to pay through the nose."
Neither is there any problem with *principal* as a noun if we recall that this noun is derived from the adjective *principal,* an adjective that means *first, foremost,* and *chief.* Thus a chief participant in a legal action became known as a *principal,* and the main actors in a drama came to be called the *principals* and none of this had anything to do with *tenet, axiom,* or *fundamental truth.* Nor did it have anything to do with a sum of money that was drawing interest down at the bank or the

chief teacher who was giving orders over at the school—both referred to as *principal*.

School administrators often have suggested that an easy way to distinguish *principle* from *principal* is to always remember that the *principal* is your *pal*—or else. Bankers, on the other hand, smirk about how the girl with the least amount of *principle* often draws the greatest amount of interest.

Q: Can you recommend a good book that deals with synonyms? Also could you tell me why there are so many words in English that mean the same thing? Take, for example, four words that you hear everyday: parasite, leech, freeloader, *and* sponger. *All of them mean the same thing. It isn't that way in Spanish, not even in Tex-Mex.*

Hortencia Quinonez
Dimmitt, TX

A: The book you're probably looking for is *Roget's Thesaurus.* As to your other question, most authorities on English vocabulary (perhaps some reader can speak about the other two languages) tell us that just about every word of the nearly million words in our language has its own excuse for being. It's rare when you can exchange one word for the other. There are few perfect synonyms.

A case in point is the four words you mention. To begin with, these four words fall into two separate sets: *parasite* and *leech* are used formally; *freeloader* and *sponger* informally. The set *parasite* and *leech* also call to mind biological organisms that attach themselves physically to a victim. *Leech* is the more pejorative term since it suggests a blood-sucking worm. Both the parasite and the leech do harm to the victim's health, sometimes enough to cause permanent damage or death. There is nothing charming about either one of them.

On the other hand, sometimes the freeloader or sponger can exude a certain amount of charm. Also these words suggest an on-again off-again relationship with the victim, a sort of hit-or-miss approach distinct from the quasi-permanent relationship that the parasite or leech establishes with the targeted prospect.

Freeloader suggests an affable guy (or girl) who is always ready to *load* up on someone else's food or booze with no thought of returning the hospitality. The word *sponger* carries a less pejorative connotation and suggests the ingratiating barfly or the one-way borrower who never returns your lawnmower or *Thesaurus.*

Q: Both rendezvous *and* tryst *mean some sort of date. But what is the difference between them, varying degrees of illegality?*

Port Robardy
Texarkana, TX

A: Date is the general term. It suggest informality ("Sue has a *date* at Hair Headquarters") or something casual ("She also has a luncheon *date* with a girlfriend"). Even when it pertains to an appointment with a member of the opposite sex, there is no suggestion of furtiveness ("College kids generally *date* on the weekend").

With *rendezvous* we usually find a hint of the amorous or the conspiratorial ("The gangsters are holding their monthly *rendezvous* at The Bloody Bucket"). But when FDR proclaimed, "This generation of Americans has a *rendezvous* with destiny," he wasn't thinking of its conspiratorial ring but of its connotative connection with duty and the military.

Tryst is basically poetic, always conspiratorial, and so charged with romantic overtones ("a *tryst* beneath the stars") that it would seem odd to find it used for other encounters. Thus, you'd never speak of a "*tryst* of trigonometry teachers," or a "*tryst* of truss-fitters." The word is aglow with moonlight and roses.

Assignation is a word that rarely has innocent overtones. Ever since George Bernard Shaw borrowed it from the French, it has suggested illicit sex in a clandestine meeting. You didn't ask about *assignation,* but it does fit climactically into the "varying degrees of illegality" you mention.

VII.

Spelling

Q: Last week I won the spelling championship of the elementary grades because I remembered "i before e except after c." But what is the rest of the poem? Next year I've got to defend my championship.

Cathi Hodges
Puyallup, WA

A: "Or when sounded like *a* as in *neighbor* or *weigh.*" As usual, there are a few exceptions. If you study the sentence "The *weird financier* will *seize either* your *friend* or your *leisure,*" you will successfully defend your crown, and should you convert it into a meaningful jingle or limerick, they may just name you "Poet Lariat of the West."

Besides being gifted with unusual visual imagery, champion spellers always have two other possessions: a willingness to work and a reservoir of such helpful hints as "I put a DENT into the superintenDENT because the princiPAL was my PAL."

Many rewards await a champion speller, rewards that transcend the championship ribbon and newspaper recognition. Words are the tools of thought, and the good speller has the key to the magical world of ideas and dreams.

Q: What is the plural form of "cupful" and "spoonful"? Is it "cupsful" or "cupfuls"? I see different spellings and never feel quite certain.

Sylvia M. LaRue
Dallas, TX

A: The plural of nouns is formed by adding *s* or *es* to the noun, and the only correct form for these two words is *cupfuls* and *spoonfuls*.

Your indecision is understandable. In the older cookbooks, both forms of the plural were sometimes used. Although these cookbook writers may have been successful in solving the gastronomical problems of early Americans, their disregard for the structure of the English language has led to many problems in spelling that will not go away. The uncertainty about *cupfuls* is one of them.

It may be helpful to remember that the plural of *quart* is *quarts,* that of a *gallon* is *gallons,* and each is a unit of measurement. *Cupful* is just another unit of measure, another noun that takes an *s* in the plural.

* * *

Letters indicate, however, that some people will cling to these ill-favored forms despite our solemn counsel.

For example, F.E. Patterson of Tyler, Texas writes:
"Referring to your article in the Sunday *Dallas Morning News:* Please correct your answer—which should be *cupsful* and *spoonsful.*
"The nouns are *cup* and *spoon,* not *ful.* "
Lois Boston of Dallas feels strongly on this subject:
"How can 'so-called' smart people give such an answer to the question about *cupsful* and *spoonsful* as you did in Sunday's paper.
"You gave the definition using *quarts* and *gallons.* How stupid!
"If there were more than one cup it would be *cups,* also *spoons,* just as you would *quarts* and *gallons,* but you would not say *quartfuls.* How silly can you get?
"There were three *quartsful.* There were three *cupsful.*
"It's the cup that is plural, not the part that is *ful.* Would you say they are *fulls?*
"Oh my!"
OK. This is not entirely a matter of opinion. Before you say more *mouthfuls,* please consult any reliable dictionary published since 1980 for the plural of the word *cupful* (which springs from the Middle English *coppefulle*).

Granted, *cupsful* does appear—as a second choice to *cupfuls*—in *Webster's Third New International Dictionary* of 1966, a book which obviously tried to please everyone and only managed to muddy this issue.

Consider then the following:

Webster's Ninth New Collegiate Dictionary (1982) says *cupfuls* only.

The new *Random House College Dictionary* (1983) says *cupfuls* only.

The new *College Edition of the American Heritage Dictionary* (1982) says *cupfuls* only.

And the venerable *Oxford English Dictionary*—the supreme court of our language (whenever it's on our side)—says *cupfuls.*

These dictionaries offer no other plural for *cupful* than *cupfuls.* Indeed, *cupfuls,* we insist, is the only correct plural.

Q: Honestly, I'm confused more than ever (apropos cupfuls, *as you advised, instead of* cupsful*). How do you handle the plural for mother-in-law?*

Does the rule apply similarly as in cupfuls?

Thanks a heapful.

Paula Olenberg
Dallas, TX

A: A rule would be useful, if anyone can find or invent one. The fact is some compound nouns are treated as simple nouns and form their plurals with a final *-s: Cure-alls, hand-me-downs, forget-me-nots.*

But others add to the most important element an internal *-s: aides-de-camp, editors-in-chief, justices of the peace.*

Still others, composed of two nouns, pluralize both nouns: *gentlemen callers, women singers, menservants.*

The reliable *Britannica Book of English Usage* (Doubleday/Britannica Books, 1980) points out:

". . . Since some compounds have two acceptable plural forms (*e.g., attorneys general, attorney generals; courts-martial, court-martials* . . .), if you are doubtful about a correct plural form,"—yes, look it up in a good dictionary.

To answer your question, we will observe that the most effective legal deterrent to bigamy is the prospect of the awesome penalty of two *mothers-in-law.*

Q: My daddy talks about "daylight savings time." But is it correct to add an "S" to "saving" in this way?

Gina Vaughn
Athens, TX

A: It's easy to add the letter *S* to this word because we're conditioned to the plural form in *savings bond, savings bank,* or the myriad other nouns in instances in which only the plural form is correct such as *news, kudos, kilts, tights,* and *potatoes* when mashed. But the only correct form in this case is *daylight saving time* because *saving* is an adjective in this expression. Probably your dad is thinking of a *savings account* like the one he's building for Christmas.

Q: I was a senior in high school before I learned that "athlete" has only two syllables, and I was a senior in college before I realized that "prostate gland" is spelled without a second "R." Before I'm a senior in grad school, I need to learn if there are any other words to which we erroneously add letters.

Billy Travis
Pilot Point, TX

A: Several. Many students are prone (or should we say "prostrate"?) to add an extra syllable to "grievous" and "mischievous" but compensate for this addition by removing the "N" from "government," the "O" from "environment," and transposing the "L" and "V" in "irrelevant."

To pronounce the "T" in "potpourri" is considered a "heinous" crime by those in the know. The first vowel in "heinous" is pronounced as the first vowel in "pain" and not as that in "pine."

Despite the ring of authority that deans give to "doctorial" as they consistently mispronounce it, dictionaries continue to spell it "doctoral" with the accent on the "doc."

Since you're entering grad school, you're obviously interested in ideas, and since you're from East Texas, you may have noticed that many people are prone (again only prone) to mispronounce "idea." They need to knock the "L" out of that word.

Q: This question concerns spelling. Is it teetotal *or* teatotal; *whiskey or* whisky? *In many legal documents you see both.*

Robert C. Crouch
Attorney-at-Law
Greenville, TX

A: Teetotal is the only correct spelling. During the temperance movement of the 19th century those who signed the abstinence pledge were entered with *O.P.* (old pledge) after their name and continued as social drinkers; but those who pledged themselves to abstain wholly from alcohol had a *T* (for total) after their signature. Thus a new word entered our language, *teetotal,* formed by reduplication of the initial letter for the sake of emphasis.

Whiskey and *whisky* are two different beverages, according to our local authority on booze, bacchanalia, and sin. *Whiskey* is Irish; *whisky* a product of Scotland. With *whiskey,* the barley is malted (allowed to germinate), then dried and mashed with water. Over in Scotland, the malt is dried over open peat-fired kilns, which (according to Dr. Renfro) gives the *whisky* its distinctive smoke taste. *Whiskey* is never admitted to the bar until it has been distilled three times and allowed to mature for several years in oak casks; in Scotland, the liquid must be blended. The Irish place great emphasis on the distilling; the Scots, on the blending.

As to which process is superior, theorists have argued for centuries. At the bar, theory gives way to practice.

Q: I am of the opinion that the plural of the word "pair" is "pairs," and it is listed that way in the dictionary. Yet I continue to see the plural listed as "pair" and also to hear it used that way in conversation.

M.C.M.
Dallas, TX

A: Your opinion is correct. "Pair" is singular while the only correct form for the plural is "pairs."

Examples: "A pair of slacks," but "three pairs of socks."

The big problem comes not so much with the noun but with the verb that follows.

"A pair of scissors *was* found at the scene of the accident." (Singular)

"Those scissors *belong* to Bob Hope, a famous cutup." (Plural)

Q: Could you help me with the spelling of two sets of words? Set one is two, to, *and* too; *the other set is* there, their, *and* they're. *Sometimes I even see* thare.

Carlton Holland
Sulphur Springs, TX

A: You are not the only one who has had problems with these words. Fortunately, some of our readers have sent us some sentences that demonstrate the correct usage.

As to the first set (*two, to,* and *too*), Bill Barnes, a nutrition expert, gives us the sage advice "Two beers are two too many to drink before breakfast." The quip of physicist Arlen Zander may elucidate further: "Clones are people two."

For the second set (*their, there,* and *they're*), the word-play of Pat Coker is priceless. "There's an inspiring interest in education among the inmates at the local penitentiary. They're all reading literature. According to their warden, however, the emphasis is on escape literature."

Now to the grammar.

Two is an adjective; *too,* an adverb; and *to,* a preposition. With the second set, the dictionary tells us that *their* is a possessive pronoun; *they're,* a contraction for *they are;* and *there,* an adverb.

Modern grammarians make a further distinction and call *there* a dummy word in this instance.

Thare is deep East Texan for all three.

Q: Would you mind explaining the difference between anymore *and* any more, *and between* anybody *and* any body?

Brandon Johnson
Sunnyvale, TX

A: Anymore is an adverb and is always used with a negative. "Ginger Rogers doesn't dance much *anymore.* " In some areas—around Pittsburgh, for example— we often hear *anymore* used in an affirmative sentence ("Ginger Rogers is sad *anymore*"), but this use of *anymore* in the sense of *nowadays* is dialectal and is traceable to the heavy influx of Scotch-Irish immigrants.

Any is an adjective. "Fred Astaire doesn't have *any more* hair."
Note how *any* is used as an adjective in the following sentence.
"Did they find *any* body in that building after the big fire?"
But *anybody* is a pronoun. "*Anybody* could have entered that building without permission."

With *anybody* or *anyone,* the rule is to combine the words to make the pronoun form and separate them if the first portion is a modifier.

Q: Last summer your paper ran a feature about an Oriental girl who won the spelling contest in Dallas. I thought no more about it until the same thing happened in California and then in Vegas. What is the story? Is it genetics? Why do Orientals do better in our schools than native-born American children?

Desiree M. Velasco
Las Vegas, NV

A: Their parents care. At least, that is one good explanation.

For decades, American parents have been shifting their responsibility from the home to teachers and school administrators.

Genetics has nothing to do with it. Time does. And Oriental parents seem willing to devote more time to the supervising of homework than do many American parents. As a result, we are going to hear a lot more valedictories from Asian students and see a lot more of them move into graduate scholarships at prestigious universities.

There have been some studies on this phenomenon, and they indicate that Americans tend to overlook the importance of family relationships in academic achievement and to overemphasize school budgets, classroom size, and building modernization.

Even though we continue to multiply mediocrity, at least more of our schools are air-conditioned.

Q: So many times I see the words "collectible," "convertible," "deductible," and many other "ible" words spelled with the "able" ending that I wonder if there is some rule that governs the correct endings of these words. I am sure that I read a rule somewhere. I intended to remember it.

Evelyn H. Wilkie
Dallas, TX

Q: I write to a girl who is both loveable and adorable. Yet I am never sure of the spelling of these "able" words. Can you give me a good working rule?

Jerry McManus
Greenville, TX

A: The suffixes of "ible" and "able" create problems because, though they are pronounced the same, they are spelled differently. Fortunately, there are a few helpful hints—three of them—that will simplify the decision as to which spelling is correct. And the first of these hints has the ring of Biblical authenticity behind it: "An *I* for an *I* and an *A* for an *A.*" If the *ible/able* adjective is closely related to a noun that ends in *ion* (*collect-ion, convers-ion, deduct-ion*), then the adjectives will end in "ible", such as the three you cited by Ms. Wilkie. On the other hand, if the *ible/able* adjective is related to a noun that ends in *ation,* then the adjective will end most likely in "able." From *adapt-ation, ador-ation,* and *applic-ation* come *adapt-able, ador-able,* and *appli-cable,* to name just a few at the beginning of the alphabet.

The dictionary tells us that there are more words ending in "able" than in "ible"; so if you are in doubt and your dictionary isn't handy, put your money on "able." After all, "able" was the basic form of "ible" and "able."

After the Bible and the dictionary comes the *Reader's Digest,* and an article from its pages tells us that "able" is added to whole words, as in the two cited by Jerry McManus (*adorable* and *lovable* from *adore* and *love*), while "ible" is added to the root or stem (*ed-ible* and *feas-ible* from "ed" and "feas").

Two other words that aptly demonstrate this dichotomy are *marriage-able* (from a whole word) and *elig-ible* (from a root), words that Jerry McManus may well be using in future correspondence—incredible and controvertible though it now may seem.

Q: As a math major with a minor in computer science, I'm trying to find some logic and consistency in English spelling, especially in the doubling of the final consonant. We double the consonant in "preferred" but not in "preference," in "stopped" but not in "stooping," in "petting," but not in "competing." I'm hoping to win the spelling contest next year. (Or am I hopping?)

Jeff Loudan
Josephine, TX

A: Doubling takes place with "pet" because it ends in a consonant, not with "compete" because it ends in a vowel. There is doubling with "stop" because it ends in a consonant preceded by only one vowel while "stoop" contains two vowels. The rule is "it must end in a consonant and be preceded by one vowel and—it must be accented." This explains why we have doubling with "preferred" and not with "preference."

If you have difficulty remembering all three parts of the rule, make up such helpful sentences as "the carpenter was busily 'planing' while his son was still 'planning,'" or "it never 'occurred' to him that he was killing not 'curing'."

With a little skill and the urging of spring any young man can construct a sentence that contrasts "petting" and "competing."

When winter comes you can construct a list of those doubled and those not. Doubled: "blotter, clannish, fatter, funnier, goddess, committed, compelling, excellent, extolling, intermittent, rebellious." Not doubled: "curing, planing, hoping, loving, appealing, benefiting, offering, proceeding, studied."

While "quitter" may seem to be an exception, it actually follows the rule because "qu" is considered one consonant by grammarians.

With the help of this rule, which applies to 3,000 words, and with the jingle "i" before "e," which controls 500 more, you should go to the state finals. And with your interest in logic and expertise in programing (or programming), you may even assemble your own language.

Exceptions to the "i" before "e" jingle appeared in this space unjingled a short time back, inspiring some readers to create some handy tools.

Mary Beth Lasater of Dallas wrote: "I look forward to your column in my newspaper each Sunday and usually learn something interesting or useful or both. Your couplet about 'i' before 'e' is the only spelling rule I know and truly a most helpful one. My sentence of exceptions, however, is different and perhaps a bit better than a list of words. I would like to share it with you: 'The weird foreigner seizes neither leisure nor sports at his height.'"

Susan Nolen of Dallas went a step beyond, adding rhyme to reason:

"Although I may not be 'poet lariat of the west,' nor a good typist, here is my contribution to the world of spelling rules:

"A *weird financier* often said, 'My *friend* must be sick in the head. He can have a *seizure,* at his own *leisure,* or *either* my eyes are misled.'

"This 'shaggy doggerel' retains the words from the original sentence, but aren't a few words what it's all about?"

Yep.

Q: In a column on spelling you stated that we should double the final consonant with "pet" (petting) because it ends in a consonant but not with "compete" (competing) because this one ends in a vowel. So far, so good. Now my students are asking me why newspapers don't double the "S" in the word "busing." Is there any special reason?

> *Ms. Mary Lou Brown*
> *Queen City, TX*

A: There are really two reasons.

One is that in the interest of space the headline writers prefer the single-consonant form; and the word "busing" has hit the headlines with consistency.

Editors also want to avert confusion with "buss," another verb and possible litigation.

"We can't keep meeting this way," said the cute secretary to the assistant principal. "I'm against school bussing unless it leads to harmonious integration."

Q: Why doesn't someone do something about spelling of English? All we have to do is to spell phonetically.

> *Sidney Craft*
> *Dallas, TX*

A: Since your letter was also phonetically addressed, it at least proves one important point: the post office has finally cracked the ZIP code. But, seriously, Sidney . . .

Once in a pale blue moon an event occurs that is so right for the time that one is struck by the Grand Design of Things. Such an event occurred in the 15th century right after the invention of the printing press. Richard Mulcaster codified the spelling of the English language so that vowels were pronounced the way they were written.

It was Utopia, euphoria and a golden age for spelling. It was also ecumenism; English vowels had the same quality as their continental cousins. Long "A" was pronounced like "A" in "father" and "E" like "E" in "there," etc.

Enter the villain.

Where he came from no one knew; in fact they didn't even know who he was. But imperceptibly the vowels began to shift, and by the time the Great Vowel Shift had ended, the long vowels of "A" and "E" and "O" had been fronted and raised in the mouth and the vowels "I" and "U" had become diphthongs. In retrospect and in comparison, the Frisco earthquake, Vesuvius, and Saturday night at Tarpley's Tavern look like trivial tremors. Because of the Great Vowel Shift, our vowel symbols no longer corresponded to the sounds they once represented and many a great intellect had trouble with spelling. If Gutenberg and Mulcaster could have waited a century or so . . .

Immediately went up the cry for spelling reform, a drastic reform, a cry that grew into a stentorian howl as it found proponents from such celebrities as Andrew Carnegie and Theodore Roosevelt plus literary giants like George Bernard Shaw and William Dean Howells, not to mention Shakespeare critics like Brander Matthews, assorted Ag majors, football coaches, strippers, and key-punch operators.

Judging from history, however, if spelling is to be reformed, it will be done gradually, with little disruption of the system and for several good reasons.

First, almost half of our words (49 percent) can be spelled correctly on a phonological basis. Second, the etymological value (derivation of words) of the old spelling is an asset not to be easily relinquished in a language as cosmopolitan as ours. If there is any international language, it is English. Third, who is to say that the sole function of writing is to reproduce sounds?

For many persons today, the written word is as important as the spoken word. With the English morphologically based spelling system (units of meaning), we can use the same "S" in "televise" as in "television," the same "I" in "divinity" as in "divine," and there is one less reason why Johnny can't spell.

If we were to reform spelling drastically, years might be needed to translate *The Hunt County Shopper,* not to mention the assorted volumes in the Library of Congress, and this monumental exertion might only, as before, end with another great vowel movement. Gradual reform is the word.

You'll need patience, Sidney. It's like waiting for an invitation to Kareem Abdul-Jabbar's retirement party.

Q: Like most physical education majors, I have trouble with English, especially speling. *Are there any good books on this subject that you could recommend? Are they very interesting?*

Troyanne Mulanax
New Diana, TX

A: Aptly, Gerald Seligman has written: "In business, spelling is one of the few skills that demand perfection. A proposal can be a few days late; a phone call returned tomorrow; a letter handed in by late afternoon; a visit postponed until next week—but for spelling there is only one expectation: IT HAS TO BE PERFECT."

Fortunately, there are a number of books that can help. Two in this field that get high ratings are Doubleday's *Spelling Made Simple* and Barron's *Business Spelling the Easy Way,* but there are scores of others. Most of them are humorless, and since none of them will ever be made into a movie, you will have to read them chapter by chapter.

Basically, all of them say the same thing:

■ That expert spellers are born, but everybody can learn how.

■ That good spellers are rewarded in the business world and bad spellers operate at a handicap.

■ That bad spellers misspell relatively few words but that these few words occur with painful frequency.

■ That 90 percent of all writing consists of about 1,000 basic words.

■ That the most frequently misspelled words are *all right, coming, receive,* and *separate.*

■ That the words most frequently confused are *its* with *it's; your* with *you're; they're* with *there* and *their;* and *to* with *too* and *two.*

■ That correct pronunciation helps to avert adding an extra *a* to *athlete,* and *i* to *mischievous, ur* to *arthritis,* while sidestepping such malapropisms as *milk of amnesia, pullet surprise,* and *Moses* on top of *Mount Cyanide.*

■ That your biggest help will come when you possess a dictionary in which you are free to write, making sure to put a mark beside the word whenever you check its spelling. On or about the 14th mark, you will have become familiar with the word, and authorities tell us that when we are familiar with the words, then we spell them correctly.

One shibboleth that separates the expert speller from the inept, according to these books, is his skill in using the apostrophe with *it's*. When wrongly tempted to insert an apostrophe in *its* to show possession, always remember that we do not use an apostrophe with *his* or *her* and that the possessive *its* falls into the same class. To show that the letter *i* is missing from *it is*, we do use the apostrophe in the contraction *it's* as in the frosty sentence culled from the book *Famous Last Words:* "It's your turn to light the fire."

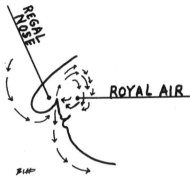

VIII.

Punctuation

Q: Would you give me a good working rule for the use of capital letters? For example, sometimes high school *is capitalized; sometimes not. Same with* middle ages, *sometimes it is capitalized, sometimes in lower case. In Germany there is no problem, according to my grandparents, because all nouns are capitalized. When did the English quit capitalizing nouns? It would be so much simpler if you could go back to that system, especially for a business major who gets graded down for incorrect use of capital letters.*

Melinda Schimmelpfennig
Greenville, TX

A: Capitalize the particular, not the general; a sentence or two will demonstrate the rule: "My sister graduated from Plano High School in 1951. While in high school, she participated in basketball, band, and fooling around."

It's the same girl, same school, but *school* is a proper noun in the first instance. Another sentence: "Women began to use cosmetics during the Middle Ages; and today women still begin to use cosmetics in their middle ages."

You may not always find a black-white dichotomy as in these sentences; so consistency is the key word in the gray areas. Have authority or argumentation for capitalizing a noun, and then stick to it.

In the field of consistency, no one can surpass the Germans, for (as your grandparents mentioned) they capitalize all nouns. Back in the 17th and 18th centuries, the English also capitalized nouns—sometimes. But they were whimsical: a noun may occur both ways in a single piece of writing from the period, often on the same page.

It wasn't until the publication of Samuel Johnson's dictionary that spelling began to be fixed. And from the middle of the 19th century until today one encounters few upper-cased common nouns—except in the writing of business majors from Texas who happen to have German ancestors.

Q: A theme with a comma splice receives an automatic "F" at many schools, this seems harsh to a farm boy.

Tom Mabe
Pecan Gap, TX

A: We note that farmer Tom subtly included a comma splice in his comment. The comma after "schools" should have been a semicolon.

The practice of rambling from one complete statement to another with only a comma keeping them apart is, according to the textbooks, a comma splice.

But what do students, administrators, and teachers think about penalizing the comma splice with a failing grade?

"If the *Gettysburg Address* contained a comma splice," asked a student, "would you slap Lincoln with an 'F,' the same grade you gave the ag major for his innocent theme, the same grade you assigned to the music major who didn't even turn in a paper? If you fail me for my use of a comma, then I'll play it safe and use mostly semicolons. But really are mechanics of saying something more important than thought or thinking?"

A coordinator of freshman composition responded, "Thought is always more important than mechanics. And since a comma splice is a symptom of disorderly thinking, we must penalize it with a—to use the euphemism—negative grade. Students who commit a comma splice lack an understanding of basic sentence structure. There's generally a lot wrong with such a theme, but here is a tangible place to start."

A former chairman of an English department pontificated: "A semicolon is trivial and in size a period is minute, but if you miss a period, it's serious. Now in an ideal world we would give no grades at all, but we are expected to prepare students for the real world by business and the military. We must not multiply mediocrity."

A chairman of an organized research department took a more avuncular approach: "After spending four years at an institution of higher education, when a student walks across the stage to receive the hearty handshake of the president, somehow we expect him to put a period at the end of a sentence . . . And yet I've seen an occasional comma splice sneak into a good paper by a student—and maybe into a mediocre speech by a president."

Truth seems to reside not in absolutes but in nuances.

The English teachers could not be reached for comment. They were correcting comma splices.

(We have had many questions about the last comma in a series. The following was selected because it came from a federal employee in Washington comma D.C.)

Q: Theoretically, the comma is supposed to take the place of the conjunction "and." Yet we see both the comma along with the "and" in the series "A,B,C, and D." What's wrong with "A,B,C and D?" I hope this question isn't too trivial.

Jerry George
Washington, DC

A: Trivial, no; confusing, yes. Actually, the answer is: it all depends. It depends on the reader or the publication you have in mind. If it is anything related to newspapers, follow the *UPI Stylebook* and delete the final comma ("A,B,C and D"). That's the rule generally (but not slavishly) followed by the newspaper editors.

In all other forms of communication, however, go ahead and use the comma ("A,B,C, and D"). It's the form preferred by the *Government Printing Office Stylebook.* But in addition to government publications—your obvious chief concern—this practice applies to all formal articles, letters of application, term papers, English themes, hijacker threats (comma?) and suicide notes. (There's no point in hunting high and low for a missing comma in a series when you could have inserted it serenely before departure.)

The argument that textbooks give for the final comma is clarity, especially when the last two items in the series could lead to ambiguity as with "coffee and doughnuts" or "bacon and eggs" or "scotch and soda" or "rice and honey." Do you dunk the doughnuts, scramble the eggs, mix the scotch or honey the rice? Only a comma can solve such a gastronomical crisis.

But the comma, that curvaceous wonder, also lends clarity in matters musical, as with the following sentence: "At the rock concert we hear Blackberry Wine, Golden Gate Bridge, Marsha Mabe and the Bulldogs." Is Marsha the leader of the Bulldogs? Do the Bulldogs even have a leader?

Your question, Jerry, isn't a triviality. We are pleased that Washington concerns itself with correctness in punctuation. Had the legislature of North Dakota displayed similar solicitude, they wouldn't have outlawed sleeping in hotels in 1929.

They only meant to curtail sleeping in restaurants (an intent that speaks unfavorably of the service in North Dakota restaurants) when they approved a measure proclaiming: "No hotel, restaurant, dining-room, or kitchen shall be used as a sleeping room by any employee or any other person."

Probably the comma-tose lawmakers meant to place a hyphen after "hotel."

Perhaps a law against sleeping in the legislature would have been more appropriate.

Architects cover their mistakes with ivy; English teachers live long enough to see theirs grow up and write laws.

Q: What's the punctuation when a dependent clause follows the main clause? I know we use a comma when the dependent clause comes first: "If you enjoy rural life, you'll love Rivercrest." But suppose the independent clause came first.

I ask this because sometimes teachers mark it wrong when I insert the comma and sometimes they don't. Also so many of the grammars sidestep the punctuation problem in this type of sentence.

Do we use a comma there or not?

Mary Fortner
Talco, TX

A: It frequently is the writer's decision, according to Professor Jan Walker who has authored many articles on punctuation. If the writer considers the dependent clause an afterthought, then he should use the comma; if not, then no comma. An example will clarify.

"I have enough money to last me the rest of my life, as long as I don't have to buy anything."

The dependent clause is an afterthought, a parenthetical addition, or in the language of the grammarian, a nonrestrictive dependent clause.

Let's look at a clear-cut example in which we do not use a comma: a restrictive dependent clause.

"We knew he was a loner when he went on his honeymoon alone."

But sometimes it's up to the writer. "Love is a transitive verb because it requires an object to complete its meaning" could have a comma before *because* or it could omit it. It's up to the writer; he must decide how much of a pause he wants there.

Some grammarians oversimplify the problem by refusing to discuss it, as you have noted in your search. However, you will find it treated very thoroughly in the *Harbrace Handbook* and in the *Random House Handbook.*

Q: Although I've never had trouble with logarithms, calculus, or computer science, one mystery that eludes me is the use of the comma in relative clauses, after the words who, which, that. My teacher always seemed to be talking about "boa-constrictor clauses," but I'm sure it was something else.

Marlene C. Carter
Garland, TX

A: Your teacher was talking about non-restrictive clauses. The best way to understand the comma in this instance is to ignore the rule and look at the examples. Note that we do not use the comma in the following sentences: "All students who misuse the comma must transfer to the University of San Salvador." "The Health Club that prefers wooden restroom seats to plastic ones is known as the Birch John Society."

But here we do use the comma: "John Jonz, who misused the comma, had to transfer to the University of San Salvador." "The John Jonz Health Club, which defers to wooden restroom seats, is known as the Birch John Society."

When we have a parenthetical clause, an afterthought that does not identify the person or thing modified, we use the comma. This is the non-restrictive clause.

Q: *Today my fourth-grade son brought home a paper in which he had been required to divide words into syllables. One of the words was "scanty" which he erred by dividing as "scan-ty." This sounded right to me; so I looked it up in my dictionary. It appears as follows: "scant-y (SCANT + Y)."*

Can this be right? And are there other words that are pronounced one way and divided into syllables another way?

Mrs. Roy D. Mims Jr.
Comanche, TX

A: Actually, both you and the dictionary are right. You are correct in breaking the word into *scan-ty* when you pronounce it, and the dictionary is accurate in reporting that the written division is *scant-y.* It must be recognized that spoken and written divisions are not the same. Dictionaries show the spoken division in the pronunciation key, but the written hyphenation in the main entry. For example, no one says *list-ing,* but that is the division on paper for the word we pronounce *lis-ting.*

The reason for this disparity is that the syllabifications used in dictionaries today are the same as those adopted by the editors back in the 18th century, syllabifications which many current editors and lexicographers consider inconsistent and illogical. But the alternative would instigate a cataclysmic revolution in printing and publishing.

There would be no problem if your son would be hyphenating *scanty* in a formal theme or a short story. This is one word you don't hyphenate. In any word where there will be a single letter on either line (*e-vade, man-y, scant-y*), grammarians tell us not to divide.

Q: There is a saying among ordnance people that the smaller the weapon the more difficult it is to control with any degree of accuracy. That seems to be the case with the hyphen. Could you give us a few simple rules? We wish that you would tell us that it is falling out of use.

Lt. Col. Kenneth Hanushek
Sulphur Springs, TX

A: Not only is the hyphen not falling out of use but there are four definite instances where we could not do without it. Please, note the following.

A: Nice girls don't enter a dirty movie theater.
B: Nice girls don't enter a dirty-movie theater.
A: Do you want to see a man eating tiger?
B: Do you want to see a man-eating tiger?
A: Our newspaper employs a thousand odd men and women.
B: Our newspaper employs a thousand-odd men and women.
A: In basketball, a big city boy has the edge.
B: In basketball, a big-city boy has the edge.

These examples demonstrate the most common use of the hyphen: to achieve clarity when two words function as one word, or when two words function as one adjective. In the sentence "They hot-roll all the metals and double-rivet the joints," we have another demonstration. Here two words function as a verb with a single meaning.

Another use of the hyphen is tied in with prefixes. You often use it with the prefixes *ex, all,* and *self* (*Ex-wife,* for example.) It is useful, too, sometimes when a woman wants to retain a vestige of her former identity as in *Kennedy-Onassis.* To our knowledge *elect* is the only suffix that is always preceded by the hyphen, as in *mayor-elect.*

A third instance of the hyphen's use concerns a means of preventing the meeting of two identical vowels (*anti-intellectual, co-owner, re-election*) or a possible misreading with the prefix *re,* (that is *re-cover* distinguished from *recover,* or *re-creation* from *recreation,* or *re-formation* from *reformation.*)

Finally, the hyphen is used between compound numbers (*twenty-one, ninety-nine*) as well as with fractions. "One-half of your teeth are in good shape. So, smile."

Q: Why do people generally say "a friend of Smith's" instead of "a friend of Smith"?

John Redard
Dallas, TX

A: You have called attention to a curious construction in the English language, the double genitive. "A friend of Smith's" is correct construction because—to quote an English authority—"when the genitive or possessive represents ownership, it keeps its form even when it follows the preposition *of.*"

Note the difference between "I received a picture of President Reagan" and "I received a picture of President Reagan's."

Note this construction also is used with the pronoun. We always say "a friend of mine, a friend of his" but never "a friend of me, a friend of him." It is a puzzling construction that is difficult to explain except through examples.

Q: What is the rule for adding an apostrophe s to the phrase "the Queen of England's nose"? Logically, it should come after Queen, since after all it is her nose and has nothing to do with the anatomy of England. What is this rule called? Am I wrong in assuming that the apostrophe is not used as much as it used to be used in our language? In my travels to Europe I've noted that the apostrophe is rarely used on the Continent.

Gwen B. Beryl
Greenville, TX

A: The rule is to place the apostrophe *s* after the last noun in a series: his mother-in-law's farm; Charles and Ernestine's mansion; Larry, Moe, and Curley's eye, ear, nose, and throat clinic.

Grammarians call it the split possessive or split genitive.

As for the apostrophe dropping out of use, there are some instances. Time was when we would write "Teachers' College" or "Doctors' Hospital." But today it is simply "Teachers College" or "Doctors Hospital." However, when the plural is indicated without the final *s,* then the apostrophe plus the letter *s* is necessary: "Children's Hospital" or "men's apparel."

You are correct when you say that the apostrophe is rarely used on the Continent, but in our English language we need it to preserve clarity. Note how the use of the apostrophe averts ambiguity in the following sentences:

A. I'd like to see our students work.

B. I'd like to see our students' work.

A. A clever cat knows its master.

B. A clever cat knows it's master.

A. The emcee stood at the door and called the guests' names as they arrived.

B. The emcee stood at the door and called the guests names as they arrived. The bloody blighters.

Q: In a recent column on the apostrophe with the possessive, you touched on many of the exceptions but somehow neglected to discuss the one that interested many of my friends who regularly go to Las Vegas, Nevada. Why do they omit the apostrophe in Caesars Palace? *Is there some special rule involved?*

Dr. Donald Caruth
Carrollton, TX

A: The only rule we could think of was the golden one: "He who has the gold makes the rule." We wrote to Mike Mecca, general manager of Caesars Palace. Even though he was tied up with preparations for a championship fight, he took time out to answer:

"When we came to Vegas to establish our hotel, we noted that most of the other casinos were working the Wild West motif to death; so we began looking for a motif that would suggest opulence. Roman decor, we thought would do the trick: a palace, waitresses in togalike costumes, parchment stationery, business cards with burnt edges. Not even the apostrophe was overlooked. Literally 'Caesar's Palace' would have suggested a palace for only one Caesar, but the omission of the apostrophe let our visitors know that everyone who entered was a Caesar. People always feel rich and generous—when they enter.

"I've never heard a complaint, not even from English teachers. After all, when money talks, nobody worries about the syntax."

Well, when we build our own hotel we may call it *Mikes Place*. But in Vegas, we have learned that the surest way to double your money is to remove it from your pocket, fold it quickly and carefully, then return it to your pocket.

IX.

Where did that expression come from?

Q: In his commentary on political tickets, Roger Mudd spoke of a kangaroo ticket, but I did not get the explanation.

Cynthia Cook
Dallas, TX

A: Kangaroo ticket can best be explained with an example. Suppose the candidate for office were a little shaky in his popularity, a real Adolph Ayatollah. He might then select as a running mate someone like Roger Staubach or Herschel Walker who might brighten up the prospects at the polls. If he did that, the candidate would have created a *kangaroo ticket,* heavier at the bottom, in this case, a lot heavier.

Q: There are quite a few people by the name of Jones who would like to know the origin of the expression "keeping up with the Joneses." Where did our fame begin?

Lawrence T. Jones III
Austin, TX

A: The expression became established with the appearance of a comic strip called *Keeping Up With the Joneses.* Created by A.R. Momand, it ran from 1913 to 1931. With the onset of the Depression, even the Joneses couldn't keep up.

Q: Please settle an argument for us. Where did hamburgers develop? In Cincinnati, Germany, or the Baltic states?

Nancy Pennington
Plano, TX

A: All three. During the Middle Ages, while traveling through the Baltic states, merchants from Hamburg learned how to scrape raw meat and season it with salt, pepper, and onion or garlic. In those days, they ate the meat raw. When their descendants settled in Cincinnati, they were cooking the beef, and by 1904 they were offering it between two halves of a bun in St. Louis. At a later date, the Kaiser invited the chef to his port city of the north "to teach hamburgers to the Hamburgers," but World War I intervened.

Another account credits a Texan with invention of the hamburger. Perhaps our readers can help us nail down that claim as fact. And who perfected the cheeseburger?

Q: My daughter Nichole wants to know why our all-American "hot dog" isn't called a "hot cow."

J. Spaulding
Denton, TX

A: The American hot dog has a German ancestor; in fact, two of them. Originally (around 1867), the larger beef frankfurter (after Frankfurt, Germany) and the smaller pork and beef wiener (*Wien* is the German spelling for *Vienna*) were two different sausages but by 1910 had combined to form the one now called the *hot dog.*

The name developed gradually. At the beginning of the century, most people suspected that dog meat constituted a large percentage of the mixed ingredients in the sausage. When a Hearst cartoonist drew a caricature of the sausage as an elongated Dachshund on a bun (as a jibe at the hot dog's popularity with German immigrants), the name *hot dog* became a verboten word with the Coney Island Chamber of Commerce. The controversy set off a new wave of unintended publicity. Enter the *Coney Island.*

Q: I have two questions about chicken-fried steak. How did it get its name and where did it start?

Judy Stehling
Arlington, TX

A: It had to do with the preparation. Like chicken, it is customarily dipped into a batter of milk, eggs, and then floured (a process altered by some chefs). The difference is that the heavier steak usually receives two applications.

The method was developed years ago when an enterprising chef discovered that lean cuts of beef would hold together better with chicken batter and that customers liked the almost pastry-like taste. The customers also liked the price, so much less expensive than filet mignon.

Maybe some of our readers know exactly when and where this entree developed. We have seen various unsupported claims. Certainly, an impressive monument is overdue for the inventor of this sublime, but often abused, dish.

Q: Are you acquainted with the term state of the art? *What is the derivation of the term and what does it mean?*

Mrs. H.S. Halebian
Dallas, TX

A: We are acquainted with the word and with its definition: "the highest level of technology in a field at a given time." We are not, however, acquainted with its origin.

One conjecture traces it to a phrase in Article, I, Section 8 of the U.S. Constitution: "The Congress shall have power . . . to promote the progress of science and useful arts . . . " But this is only conjecture. It is just as likely that it is a spinoff from the phrase *state-of-the-union message* since *state-of-the-art* is frequently used as an adjective.

The expression isn't new. Defense contractors have been using it for several decades.

Q: A few days ago, I again heard someone use the saying, "The exception proves the rule." I must confess that I have never understood this saying. To me, it seems illogical and contradictory. Why should an exception prove the rule? Any explanation?

Ben Swearington
Lewisville, TX

A: You are on the right track, Ben. *Prove* here doesn't mean *to confirm* but *to test;* in other words, that which doesn't conform to the rule forces us to examine the rule. As every reader of the *Bible* knows, when the Apostle Paul wrote "*Prove* all things; hold fast to that which is good," he was telling the Colossians to examine, to scrutinize, to test.

As every student of linguistics knows, when Junius Columella coined the expression, "The exception proves the rule," ("exceptio probat regulam") back in 66 B.C., the first meaning of the Latin verb *probare* was *to test.*

Q: Would you correct this rhyme for me: "Vice is a monster of evil face, which we repulse and then at last embrace." Also who is the author of the short story Shadows on the Wall? *It tells about people who spent their whole life watching shadows on the wall, and when they are taken out into the real world they reject it and return to the shadows.*

Mrs. James Berry
Kempner, TX

A: The verse is from Alexander Pope's *Essay on Man:*

Vice is a monster of so frightful mien
As to be hated, needs only to be seen;

Yet seen too oft, familiar with her face,
We first endure, then pity, then embrace.

The story is *The Wind in the Rose-bush* by Mary Wilkins Freeman and can be found in the *American Short Story Series*. It is quite possible that this motif may appear in other stories. It has soooooo many echoes of Plato.

Q: One phrase that has bothered me—long before I joined the Corps— was "tell it to the Marines." This seems to imply that the members of this organization are not only a little slow mentally but also unusually gullible, an unkind aspersion when you recall that the Marine Corps is older than other branches of the armed forces and even older than the United States itself.

Captain Dickie Lee Fox, USMC
Athens, TX

A: It is true that the marines in this aphorism are delineated with many of the earmarks of the stereotyped "Aggie," but the sea-soldiers in question here aren't the marines from Quantico or San Diego but those from Southhampton, London, and Bath—the British.

For centuries the Limey marine was the butt of many a cruel jest not only because his duties often were limited to the routine chores of military policemen, but also because the average rookie selected for the marines in England wasn't always what might be called a teeming tome of erudition. Rightly or wrongly, he was considered to be somewhat on the gullible side. Toward the end of Chapter 13 in *Redgauntlet,* Walter Scott has one character exclaim: "Tell that to the marines, the sailors won't believe it." Byron has a similar statement in *The Island* (Canto Two).

In other words, the British were *telling it to the marines* before anyone *told it* to United States Marines—although sailors of the U.S. Navy may find that incredible.

* * *

Our explanation stimulated too many letters to be published here, but several are difficult to ignore.

Brigadier General E.H. Simmons, director of U.S. Marine Corps History and Museums, wrote from Washington, D.C.:

"Your explanation of 'Tell it to the Marines' is one way of telling it. But to turn a jeer into a boast, here's how we tell it, or better, here is how Texas' own Col. John W. Thomason, Jr., famed Marine writer and artist, told it in *Fix Bayonets!* (Charles Scribner's Sons, 1925 and 1955):

In Charles the Second's time, the English formed the first sea regiment—soldiers equipped as infantry, to serve on the sea in the fleet; to clear with musketry the enemy's decks and fighting-tops when the ships of the line went into close action; to go ashore and take up positions when the naval forces would seize a base preliminary to land operations of the army.

Here, by the way, comes the quip of old time: "Tell it to the Marines." They relate of Charles the Second that at Whitehall a certain sea-captain, newly returned from the Western Ocean, told the king of flying fish, a thing never heard in old England. The king and the court were vastly amused. But, the naval fellow persisting, the Merry Monarch beckoned to a lean, dry colonel of the sea regiment, with a seamed mahogany face, and said, in effect: "Colonel, this tarry-breeks here makes sport with us stay-at-homes. He tells us of a miraculous fish that forsakes its elements and flies like a bird over the water!" "Sire," said the colonel of Marines, "he tells a true thing. I myself have often seen those fish in your Majesty's seas around Barbados." "Well," decided Charles, "such evidence cannot be disputed. And hereafter, when we hear a strange thing, we will tell it to the Marines, for the Marines go everywhere and see everything, and if they say it is so, we will believe it!"

"This version supposedly is based on an entry in Samuel Pepys' *Diary* but we wouldn't want to pursue a good thing too far, would we?"

General Simmons has the generally accepted version of the origin of the phrase. Thomason's account is repeated in *The Marine Officer's Guide* by Col. Robert D. Heinl, Jr., USMC (Ret.). A copy of it was sent to us by Marine enthusiast W.R. (Billy Bob) Crim of Kilgore.

Responding to the assertion in the column by Captain Dickie Lee Fox, USMC, of Athens, Texas, that the Marine Corps is older than the United States, Army Col. Odus C. Kerley (Ret.) of Dallas writes:

"Please know that the Army of our country is the oldest and senior service. The Continental Congress created the Continental Army June 14, 1775. Before this American colonial troops fought in the French and Indian War.

"It was not until Nov. 10, 1775, when the Continental Congress established the Marine Corps, which was created to fight in the Revolutionary War after which no Marine Corps, as such, existed. Congress re-created the Corps as a military service in 1798 . . . In 1789 Congress established the War Department to direct military affairs. This was nearly 10 years before the re-creation of the Marine Corps.

"In 1834, Congress placed the Marine Corps directly under the Secretary of the Navy. There is a great difference in a corps and an army. Our Army has in its organization many corps."

Yes, sirs.

Q: *What is the meaning and origin of "root, hog, or die"? It sounds almost Shakespearean.*

Bob Glenn
Director
Shakespeare Festival of Dallas, TX

A: We traced it to several dialect dictionaries (California, Virginia, East Alabama), which translated it into "Work or perish" or "Look out for yourself or die."

It became popular throughout the entire nation in 1944 with the appearance of a book, *The American Character,* by Sir Denis Brogan. The book received rave reviews and popular approval on both sides of the Atlantic.

Sir Denis wrote: "A people that has licked a more formidable enemy than Germany or Japan, primitive North America . . . a country whose national motto has been 'root, hog, or die' . . ."

The saying seems to have originated as the refrain in *The Bull-Whackers' Epic* which appeared in J.H. Beadle's *Life in Utah* around 1870.

> Oh, I'm a jolly driver on the Salt Lake City line,
> And I can lick the rascal that yokes an ox of mine;
> He'd better turn him out, or you bet your life I'll try
> To sprawl him on the ox-bow—Root hog, or die . . .

This refrain occurs eight times.

Shakespeare had many earthy expressions, but this wasn't one of them. We checked the concordance.

* * *

Unlike participation in such pastimes as roller derbies and wet T-shirt contests, the lively pursuit of language on the wing can be indulged gracefully from childhood into the maturing years. As proof, here is a delightful letter from Mrs. J.P. Goodman, an 85-year-old reader in Clarksville, Texas:

"Dear *Few Words* People:

"I've always been interested in words. So I have a few words about a recent column of yours devoted to the expression 'root, hog, or die.'

"In the early days, I would hear it spoken that way. (I was born in 1898.) But most often it was 'root, pig, or die pore.'

"Many of the settlers on the plains came from the Old South during the hard times following the Civil War; many came as children. And none of them (I really should say none of *us*) needed to have the expression explained. They had brought it with them, and it still fitted the difficulties of sustaining life in a hard country.

"I am glad you mentioned sources from Virginia, Alabama and California. It sounds as though the idea migrated southward and westward along with many others. It's easy to see how the expression would start where there were trees, bushes, creeks and river bottoms, because the hogs were most often left to run out and feed off the *mast*. (That meaning for that word I learned as a child from the older people.)

"Those hogs had to work at finding enough to eat. Nobody fed them. And for humans, as well as for hogs, when times were so hard and cruel, it was work desperately hard, depend on yourself, or die 'pore' of starvation, emaciated as well as 'poor.'

"Now that word 'pore' I found once in the Middle English. Isn't that how it came into our language?

"The book *Lamb in His Bosom,* by Carolyn Miller (late 1930s or early 1940s, best I remember), is set in the Old South, long ago, among the poor and uneducated in very hard times. About half the book is written in the vernacular, and it is most interesting. I copied a part of one paragraph: 'Ma said nobody fought death as hard as a mother did who left children behind her to *root-pig-or-die-pore* in a hard old world.'

"Wish I could read that book again. Would also like to go back to school and attend Dr. McNamee's classes. But probably it's a little late for both wishes. Thank you for your 'Few Words' and your attention to mine."

Q: Where can we find the origin and meaning of the phrase toe the mark?
Nocona Turf Supplies
Nocona, TX

A: In *Heaven to Betsy,* Charles Funk explains both meaning and origin: "To conform with the rules or standards of discipline; to fulfill one's obligations; to come up to scratch. Literally, this used to be a term in footracing, now replaced by the command 'take your mark,' an order to all entrants to place the forward foot on the designated starting line . . . The earliest use thus far found is in James K. Paulding's *The Diverting History of John Bull and Brother Jonathan* (New York, 1813)."

Q: My granddaughter and I would like to know where the expression foot the bill *comes from. It seems a silly way to say you will pay the check.*

Dorothy Iglehart and Amy Bradley
Dallas, TX

A: Foot has other meanings besides *pedal extremity.* We speak of "the foot" of a mountain or "at the foot of the cross" because we are speaking of the bottom part, the lower end. And since the bill comes at the lower end of the page, he who pays it, foots it. You may hear the expression also in the meaning of "pay the consequences," but here *foot* is used metaphorically.

Q: What is a white elephant?

Nelda Winkle
Winnsboro, TX

A: A white elephant is any expensive item that is useless to the owner, costly to maintain, and impossible to get rid of.

The phrase goes back to the reverence attached to the albino elephants in the ancient kingdom of Siam. It was sacrilegious to work them, and they could not be disposed of or destroyed without permission of the king. So whenever the king was displeased by some courtier, he would *honor* him with a gift of a voracious white elephant, which would eventually bankrupt the unfortunate courtier—even if he had an organic garden.

Q: I would like to know the measurements for a rick of wood, and how many ricks are in a cord. I have heard many different measurements for this, and I wonder if it varies in different localities.

Martha Lowe
Dallas, TX

A: There should be 128 cubic feet in a cord. It is 4 feet high, 16 feet long, with each piece of wood measuring out at 2 feet. A rick is half a cord: 4 by 8 by 2 feet. These dimensions don't vary from locality to locality, supposedly.

What does vary is the *face cord* or *face rick,* when the length of wood is determined by the dimensions of the stove, the wishes of the consumer, or the eccentricity of the supplier. It may be 20 inches long, say, or 18. A term in use now in Dallas is the *bundle* which contains 1.15 cubic feet.

Freezing people sometimes complain about the cost of a rick of wood, but, when you put a sharpened pencil to it, you will find that it is no more expensive per cubic foot than a good piano.

Q: Why do we say "knock on wood"? I've heard it for years.

Frank Hodges
Irving, TX

A: It goes back many years, in fact to the days of primitive tree worship. Knocking on wood was thought to summon up the friendly spirit who lived there in order to win his friendship.

Q: Why do we say "God bless you!" or "Gesundheit!" or something of that sort after a sneeze? What is it about a sneeze that elicits that sort of reaction?

Dr. Selig J. Kavka of Chicago has admirably summed up the situation in the Journal of the American Medical Association, *to wit: "No routine comment is invited by someone belching, coughing, groaning, retching, snorting, vomiting, wheezing, or sniffing, even when those symptoms portend trouble." But why? Why is the sneeze singled out?*

Maybe a little mystery adds seasoning to life.

Louis Cashman
Editor, Vicksburg Evening News
Vicksburg, MS

A: It all goes back to the age of otherworldliness. There was a belief that the breath of man contained his spirit, his soul. Whenever you sneezed in those days there was danger of not only expelling your soul but also of permitting evil spirits to enter and occupy the resultant vacuum. Fortunately, Providence could intervene and avert this disaster if a bystander would mutter a prayer—"God bless you!"

So much for the origin of "God bless you!" in England. How "Gesundheit!" (the German word for *health*) developed we do not know at the moment, but the German ambassador in Washington is researching the matter for us. We suspect it has something to do with onomatopoeia. Do you agree?

Q: How long have we had the expression "that's not to be sneezed at"? My interpretation is that it refers only to significant remarks or events. Inversely, it implies that insignificant remarks or events should be sneezed at. Now my life is full of a myriad of insignificant remarks or events so that to comply, I would be sneezing forever. I find it difficult to crank out sneezes at will. How far do sneezes go?

T.M. Lamb
Grand Prairie, TX

A: "To regard as of little value, worth, or consideration; to despise, disregard, underrate" is the definition given by the *Oxford English Dictionary.* It also informs us that the expression was used back in 1823: "A handsome girl with a few thousand pounds tacked to her posterior is not to be sneezed at."

Our ballistics expert informs us that the droplets of moisture in a sneeze travel at a rate of 150 feet a second and land as far away as 12 feet. Comin' right achoo!

Q: What is the origin of the term skid row? *You read it in a lot of short stories today.*

Daphne Polk
Fort Worth, TX

A: Back in the 19th century when Henry Yesler, a pioneer in the Northwest, established one of the first timber processing plants in the Seattle area, he constructed a crude road to skid logs from a landing on Elliot Bay to his sawmill. Because the timber business was both seasonal and cyclical, unemployed lumberjacks found the well-traveled thoroughfare a natural loitering place. As bars and brothels began to spring up (to keep the boys off the street), the avenue developed its unsavory reputation.

Today, Yesler Way is a major thoroughfare in downtown Seattle, but the appellation *skid row* is applied to any dilapidated area where dirty hotels are populated by unemployed poets and unemployable derelicts.

Q: I've been wanting to ask this question since the after-Christmas sale of dry goods. Why are they called dry goods? *Did they ever have any wet ones? Also why are some wines called* dry wines?

James Griffitt
Bailey, TX

A: Dry goods stores take their name from stores run by New England shipowners, many of whom were also merchants during our early history. The two chief imports in the "department store" of those days were calico and rum, discreetly displayed on opposite sides of the store: a dry goods side holding calico, the wet goods side holding you-know-what. With the influx of Irish immigrants in the 19th century, the term "wet goods" disappeared from our language. The goods joined the Micks and mixed in the saloon across the street.

"A wine without noticeable sweetness where essentially all fermentable sugar has been converted into alcohol is called a dry wine," according to Dr. Roy Renfro, the local authority on wine, brine, and turpentine. "Dry wines range from 9 to 14 percent in alcoholic content and are measured on an Oechsle Scale, a scale which determines the amount of sugar in the grape."

Q: In 30 years of teaching, I have been subjected to the expression by and large *many times. College professors, superintendents of schools, principals, and fellow teachers use the expression regularly. I detest it! What is its origin? By what? How large?*

Ralph Meyer
David Carter High School
Dallas, TX

A: It's a cliché that has lost its original meaning, has become only a conversation filler, and the pet peeve of many of the linguists we consulted. Originally sea jargon, it goes back to the days when ships were powered by sail. The *Dictionary of English Idiom* reports that it was an order to a helmsman "to keep the ship at a course it was sailing and at the same speed even though the wind was changing."

The expression has never been popular in England. According to Sir Ernest Gowers, "this usage . . . exasperates sailors."

Bergen Evans calls the expression "meaningless." It is still used, however, but by and large only by second-rate writers.

X.

Words: New,
easily confused,
and hard-to-find

Q: Several years ago while writing sports here in Pittsburgh, I was offered a job in public relations at a college in Texas.

Now nothing flatters a man more than a job offer unless it is a job offer that includes a chance to arrange employment for his wife in the same vicinity. However, when I inquired about Dorothy's working at this institution, the athletic director said: "Not a chance. You see we have the fornication law here, and the dean always enforces it."

Naturally I didn't take the job since our marriage has been a very happy one—but I've sometimes wondered about that offer.

Bill Heyman
Emsworth, PA

A: We've had several questions along this line, but we haven't been able to locate the law-abiding athletic director nor his dean of fornication.

Undoubtedly, the practice under discussion was supposed to be *nepotism,* that is to say the preference shown to relatives by those who award favored positions.

In order to avoid accusations of nepotism, the administrations of some prestigious universities frown upon the hiring of the spouse or relative of anyone on the staff.

The word originated during medieval times when a prelate could pass a bishopric or political plum to his *nepos,* the Latin word for nephew.

The word *fornication* also goes back to the Latin, but to an entirely different root: *fornax* (the furnace).

In some states, there *are* laws regarding fornication, but they aren't normally aimed at those legally married.

Athletic directors are referred to remarks by Montreal center fielder Ron LeFlore in a recent issue of *Newsweek's* magazine *Inside Sports:* "Some guys need amphetamines to get up for a game. For me, sex does it."

Whether sex "does it" for deans or doesn't has been a matter of dormitory conjecture for generations.

Q: On a recent trip to New York City I heard kids talk about "Chisanbop." Lacking the urbanity of these slickers, I felt too timid to inquire what sort of dance this was. My mother used to be a good dancer, but never did the "Chisanbop." And Daddy couldn't even find it in the dictionary so he told me to write to you.

Shelby Johnson
Bonham, TX

A: "Chisanbop" concerns not the feet, but the fingers. It is an educational method created by Sung Jin Pai, a Korean mathematician, and then modified for children by his son. The word means "finger calculation method." But it's more than just counting on your fingers.

Enthusiasts cite Chisanbop as a breakthrough comparable to jet-propulsion and computer printouts, rolled into one.

Teachers attribute much of its success to the fact that three senses are employed—sight, hearing, and touch—and in a natural fashion.

"It's a crutch," concedes Ms. Joane Walvoord of Commerce, "and when a crutch is no longer needed, it's set aside. Eventually the child performs the finger problems mentally."

Students like Chisanbop not only because it's fun, not only because it gives them confidence but because it leads them into the magical world of quantitative romance and intellectual development. Students in special education often were unable to do add-in problems in the B.C. era (Before Chisanbop).

As for administrators, they couldn't be happier: Chisanbop is inexpensive, and it keeps the kids quiet.

Q: I have a question concerning "aragula." Whatever it means, it has something to do with a salad. I ran across it in the book The Cradle Will Fall, *and have looked for it in many dictionaries without success.*

Vivian Brunk
Hamilton, TX

A: It is an Italian green, and is supposed to have a taste unique among salad greens. Described as "meaty and spicy," it is the subject of an informative article in the May 1984 issue of *Organic Gardening.*

Q: Could you please tell me a word coined by Prince Charles, I believe, a few years ago for the art of "putting your foot in your mouth." I thought it was very clever but can't remember that exact word. It was something like pedidontitis.

Mrs. J.H. Jones
Dallas, TX

A: In a letter dated June 21, 1982 (the birthdate of Prince William), Prince Charles informed us that the word in question was *dontopedology.* He added, however, that the word was not of his coinage but "the brainchild of my father, the Duke of Edinburgh."

A hybrid word, it is derived from the Greek word for tooth (*odous*), the Latin word for foot (*pes*), and the Greek word for study (*logos*). A *dontopedologist* would be one who studies putting a foot in one's mouth. *Dontopedology* is evidence that the English language is a going concern: new words are coined every day and the moribund are often revived. The survival of a new word depends in a large part on the need that it fills. It also helps if a head of state plays a role in the minting process.

In 1872, a distinguished American scholar labeled the verb *belittle* "incurably vulgar" and made a serious effort to kill it. But the word survived not only because it filled a lacuna but also because it had been coined by President Thomas Jefferson.

Normalcy had been around long before 1920, but once it was used by Warren Gamaliel Harding it took on a life of its own.

In a *Saturday Evening Post* story of 1910, novelist George Fitch used *brain trust,* and that was the last time we heard of it for 22 years until it was used in reference to three Columbia profs who were helping Franklin D. Roosevelt with his speeches. FDR liked the term, and as his popularity increased so did the popularity of *brain trust.*

John Foster Dulles not only popularized *brinkmanship;* he coined it.

Endorsement by a celebrity doesn't insure a word's longevity or even its survival. In his novel *Tancred,* Benjamin Disraeli wrote, "Lady Constance guanoed her mind by reading French novels." But even though Disraeli was prime minister, the word *guano* wasn't accepted as a verb.

Dontopedology is a long word, but *Prince William Arthur Philip Louis* is a long name. Long live them both—and innovative language.

Q: Could you run a column on the origins of maverick, posh, hooker, *and* by hook and crook?

Ray Green, Publisher
The Gilmer Mirror,
Gilmer, TX

A: Back in the days of the roaming buffalo, the playing antelope and the undug posthole, Texas cowmen traditionally branded calves in order to designate their ownership. But rancher Sam Maverick refused to do any branding, claiming that his cattle easily could be identified because they carried no brand at all. He reasoned, naturally, that any unbranded animal belonged to him. Maverick became wealthy and eventually mayor of San Antonio. Today *Maverick* still means unbranded—a nonconformist, a free spirit, even a stormy petrel.

As to *posh,* one school maintains that it is the acronym for "port out starboard home," referring to the shady side of ships of the P&O Line plying the Red Sea with passengers en route from India to England. The word generally came to mean something luxurious. Other philologists doubt this story and point out that the word never occurred in P&O records. Incidentally, the use of *posh* is discouraged by editors of *The Dallas Morning News.* Not only is *posh* imprecise but it tends to become addictive to writers and monotonous to readers. It is one of those words like *very* that usually should be left to licensed hypnotists.

A basic duty of a commanding officer is to provide his troops with food, clothing, and shelter. But a Union general, Joe Hooker, sensed a fourth need—ladies of undemanding virtue. Word historians agree that the word *hooker* goes back to General Joe. Military historians also agree that his troops manly performances seldom extended to the battlefield. Nowadays, we are told that a Hookers Ball is held annually in San Francisco. Dress is optional.

Although the term *by hook or crook* means rightfully or wrongfully, originally it pertained to procuring wood from the forest with two tools. In medieval times, the lord of the manor frequently would permit the peasants to obtain wood from his forests. What they couldn't reach with a hook, they tried to pull down with a crook. The French equivalent was *a droit ou a tort.*

Q: What is the word that describes the slatted porch so common in Texas? The slats are often used to support grapevines or something similar.
Kathy Collins
San Antonio, TX

A: The word you are looking for is *pergola.* It is derived from the Latin noun *pergula* which means "protective cover or outside workshop." Pliny also used it in the meaning of *"outhouse* utilized for various purposes," but without the current connotation.

Q: What is a YAP? *I've seen the word in print but cannot find it in the dictionary. I don't know if I would recognize one if I saw a real one.*
Terrie Bradshaw
Cooper, TX

A: YAP is an acronym for *young aspiring professionals.* They are easy to recognize: their Nike running shoes blend with their business suits.

According to C.E. Crimmins' *YAP Handbook*, there are many telltale signs of YAPiness, such as the place of work, investments, and mating instincts.

Earning no less that $50,000 a year, the typical YAP carries seven credit cards and invests heavily in condominiums with exposed brick wall and kitten to match the decor.

Unless deterred by burnout, YAPs eventually enter into a two-career marriage, and after PAPAbility teach their YAPlings both beginning French and advanced calculus so that they will be accepted by the day care center of choice.

The YAPs might be confused with the YUPPIE supporters of disappointed Democratic presidential candidate Gary Hart. YUPPIES were defined in *The YUPPIE Handbook* by Marrissa Piesman and Marilee Hartley:

"Hot new name for Young Urban Professional, a person of either sex who meets the following criteria: 1) resides in or near one of the major cities; 2) claims to be between the ages of 25 and 45; 3) lives on aspirations of glory, prestige, recognition, fame, social status, power, money, or any and all combinations of the above; 4) anyone who brunches on the weekend or works out after work."

Few, if any, YUPPIES have been seen since the Hart failure. Those who survived the campaign may have changed their names.

Currently found in the "Fastrack" comic strip of this newspaper are organized *YUMPIES*, who describe themselves as not only "young and upwardly mobile professionals" but "radically trendy and proud of it." Always with us are the *PREPPIES*, who are those people who are always in line ahead of you at any good restaurant. They are epitomized, of course, by Captain Preppy in this newspaper's "Crock" comic strip.

Perhaps the best way to define YAPs, YUPPIES, YUMPIES, and PREPPIES is to describe what they are not. They are not *YIPPIES*.

Q: What's the little plastic tip on shoelaces called? And where do you find answers to such questions?

Ron Parham
Dallas, TX

A: Aglet. We found it in Paul Dickson's *Connoisseur's Collection of Old and New and Wonderful Words.*

Q: Since Libya is so much in the news, what is the correct spelling of the name of their leader? The press has it Qaddafi, Khadafy, *and* Gaddafi. *Which one is approved by the Libyans?*

Rhome Tyree
Longview, TX

A: Ghaddafi. That is according to our man in Tripoli, Dr. Salem Ahmet. The confusion understandably arises when attempting to transliterate from the Arabic alphabet to the Roman. But you don't have to go to Africa to encounter this problem. There are six different spellings for the lake we Texans call *Tawakoni.*

Q: Last week I read about a "rising young Turk" who was being "Shanghaied." The nationality of the man was not Turkish nor was the destination anywhere in China. What do we call this misuse of language?

Dana Hendrix
San Antonio, TX

A: The word you are looking for is *eponym,* the linguistic phenomenon that takes place when the names of people or places give rise to new words. It is quite legitimate and took place long before 1908, when a group of insurgents reformed the Ottoman Empire, or the mid-19th century when country boys sometimes were kidnapped on their first visit to the city and found themselves soon on sea duty in China.

Allan Wolk's *Everyday Words* tells how Amelia Jenks campaigned for women's right to wear trousers. A new word was added to our language when she married an attorney named Bloomer. James A. Ruffner's *Eponyms* gives 730 pages explaining how words like *leotard, Judas, Svengali,* and *Xanthippe* became part of our language.

Q: As a translator, I frequently come across unusual words, but in every case the English-Chinese dictionary has helped me. Except in one case; the word is chunnel. *This must be a new word, a very new word.*

Julie Fang
Greenville, TX

A: Actually the idea goes back to Napoleon, who first proposed a tunnel under the English Channel that would connect France with Britain. You see *chunnel* in the news a lot today because they're hoping to have it completed by 1993.

Words made up of parts of other words are called *blendwords* or *portmanteau terms*, the latter coined by Lewis Carroll to designate a word like his *slithy* (a combination of *slimy* and *lithe*). Long before Carroll there were words like *gerrymander* (an 1812 combination of *Gerry* and *salamander*) and *splutter* (compounded from *splash* and *sputter*).

In more recent times, gossip columnist Walter Winchell gave birth to *infanticipating;* a Californian wheezed *smog,* and Pennsylvanians first checked out *motels.*

The number grows every day with industry extruding *thinsulation* and farmers gushing *fertigation. Medicaid* is another, and *travelog* and *cablegram.*

And, by all means, Julie, let's do *brunch.*

Q: Lately there has appeared in editorial columns the word gridlock, *which I have not found in my various word sources. It would be appreciated if you can provide the meaning.*

Hannah H. Hochman
Dallas, TX

A: Gridlock is defined as "a massive automobile traffic jam in which no car can move in any direction." (A synonym might be North Central Expressway in Dallas.) The reason for your frustration in finding it is that it has not yet appeared in many dictionaries. Our source was the book *8500 Terms Not Yet in Standard Dictionaries,* published by Mager in 1982.

According to another source, children have been born "out of gridlock" when the taxi has been delayed longer than "expected."

Q: What does this word smurf *mean that we read about so much. Is it a good word?*

Sandy Purifoy
Greenville, TX

A: A *smurf* is a courier who profits by laundering dirty money. The *smurf* makes it difficult for law enforcers or tax agents to trace "hot" money from criminal sources or money illegally obtained by racketeers. For example, the *smurf* may buy cashier's checks in amounts small enough to escape notice of banking officials. Big transactions must be reported under the Bank Secrecy Act.

A *smurf* tries to look like one of the bank's local customers or a successful businessman. A busy *smurf* may earn $1,000 a day before going to jail. Since illegal drug sales involve billions of dollars each year, it's not surprising that you see the word *smurf* in current periodicals, even in the conservative *Wall Street Journal.*

As to its origin, *smurf* comes from a little cartoon character in the funny papers.

Smurf is a useful word and a good one. But one may argue that every working word is a good word.

Q: *What is that word that means "persons of opposite sex sharing living quarters"? Could you also give the poem that your newspaper once printed?*

Berry L. Barnes
Houston, TX

A: The word is POSSLQ, and is pronounced poss-ul-cue. Here is most of the poem, which is by Charles Osgood:

> Come live with me and be my love
> And we will all the pleasures prove . . .
> . . . And everything we will confess;
> Yes, even to the IRS.
> Someday, on what we both may earn,
> Perhaps we'll file a joint return.
> You'll share my pad, my taxes joint.
> You'll share my life—up to a point!
> And that you'll be so glad to do,
> Because you'll be my POSSLQ.
>
> Come live with me and be my love,
> And share the pain and pleasure of
> The blessed continuity,
> Official POSSLQuity.
> And I will whisper in your ear
> That word you love so much to hear.
> And love will stay forever new,
> If you will be my POSSLQ.

Osgood shall be applauded–especially for his restraint in not attempting to conform the incongruity of promiscuity to the ambiguity of POSSLQuity.

Q: Recently I saw the word "mingle" used as a noun. Was this an isolated instance or is this word coming into our language? Incidentally, what is a mingle?

Denny Perkins
Dallas, TX

A: This was not an isolated use of the word "mingle." There are many mingles, close to two million mingles in the United States. And the number has doubled in the last decade, according to the U.S. Bureau of the Census.

Mingles are neither singles nor couples nor traditional roommates. They are a new brand of home owners and home sharers. They are generally young professional people who, finding the rising cost of living has outpaced their salaries, have agreed to sacrifice a modicum of privacy for a maximum of the good life, whether that means a better neighborhood, a more luxurious apartment, or just more cash in the bank.

Shelter takes the biggest bite from the budget, we are told. Mingles divide and conquer. Compatibility seems to be the key ingredient and a willingness to sit down, talk about it and write a detailed contract. The contract involves not only the equity each will have in the townhouse or apartment but also the means of splitting up any profits from the sale. Good friends rarely succeed as roommates and only in exceptional cases make it as mingles. But this is nothing new. Roommates have been bickering ever since Adam and Eve checked out the bridal suite in the Paradise Motel.

The noun "mingle" has adjusted well into our language and will eventually be accepted by the dictionary, just like "posslq." It will take time: as preachers have noted, sin has always moved faster than syntax.

Q: Is there a town called Tightwad? Some of my friends have facetiously suggested that I open a bank account in this Missouri community. I checked the zip code directory and could not find one. I even called Kansas City, and was told there is no Tightwad Bank in Kansas City. Same for Springfield. It's supposed to be a famous bank.

Virginia Richardson
Rowlett, TX

A: Yes, Virginia. There is a Tightwad Bank.

But it is neither in Kansas City nor in Springfield. It's about halfway between them. You are correct that it doesn't have its own zip code, but if you are interested in opening an account there (and more than 100 out-of-staters do have accounts at the Tightwad Bank), address your mail to Tightwad Bank, Tightwad, Missouri, 64735.

The bank came by its name honestly. Years ago, a country store was located at the site. Whether justified or not, the establishment became known locally as an enterprise that gleefully would stoop to cheating orphans and foreclosing on widows. The emporium eventually became known as "the tightwad store." The crossroads on which it was located came to be called "Tightwad Junction." After the building of the Truman Dam, increased population brought about a need for a bank. "What better name could we get than Tightwad Bank?" said a local businessman. "It would not only reflect our prosperity but should also induce frugality and stimulate the economy."

The name attracted tightwads from all over, bringing in more than half a million dollars in out-of-state accounts.

We learned that an open house has been scheduled for this weekend at the Tightwad Bank. Those who wish to attend might be well advised to bring their own refreshments.

Q: The word maven *is used in writing and now on television commercials. It apparently is a synonym for* fan, devotee, connoisseur. *Despite working in a library and looking in the standard dictionaries, I have not found it. Can you give its origin and meaning?*

Doris Chipman
Dallas, TX

A: Maven comes from the Hebrew verb *mayveen* which means "to understand." From there it was taken over by Yiddish as *maven* with the meaning of "buff" or "self-styled expert." A *shmexpert*. You can find a discussion of the word in Wentworth and Flexner's *Dictionary of American Slang*. Another one of our sources told us that it has been around for more than 30 years and has frequently been used in the garment industry.

Q: This is the second letter I have written about this word redux. *I can't find it in any dictionary, including my* Webster's Third International, unabridged. *I have seen it in* The Wall Street Journal, *in a few other places, and once in a political cartoon. What, exactly, does it mean —and where does it come from?*

Walter Bodger
Richardson, TX

A: Redux has been around a long time. It was frequently used by both Ovid and Vergil, which may explain why you don't find it in the English dictionaries. It translates "a bringing back," especially "the bringing back of a leader from exile." *Dux* means "the leader"; *redux* "the return of the leader." (*Il Duce* was a cognate term.)

Since the return-of-the-leader theme is basically archetypal (the comeback of Sugar Ray or Beowulf's fight with the dragon), every culture has its own word for this idea. Its omission in English can be explained by the fact that we have been freeloading on Latin for many centuries. This is evidenced in the title of John Updike's novel *Rabbit Redux*.

Q: I have a question about a single word and hope you can help me. What is a felon called who invades graves, tombs, or crypts to remove valuables from the dead for personal gain; and with what crime would he be charged when apprehended?

Rochelle Canon
Sherman, TX

A: The miscreant in this case is called a *ghoul.* When apprehended, he would be charged with desecration of a venerated object or abuse of a corpse. (Sections 42.09 and 42.10 respectively of the Texas Penal Code.) An offense under either section is a Class A misdemeanor.

Q: How did Tombstone, Arizona get its name? Were tombstones first used in its famous Boot Hill Cemetery?

Jimmie Finnie
Sulphur Springs, TX

A: According to an article in the local newspaper (aptly named the *Tombstone Epitaph*), the community received this unusual appellation in 1879 from Ed Schieffelin, a successful silver miner. Two years earlier he had been warned that his mine would be his tombstone because of the nearby Apaches.

As to when tombstones were first erected, we could not unearth. But from our local trivia authority, Maurice Glazer we learned that the original purpose of the tombstone was not to mark the grave but to weigh down the earth so that the deceased could not return and harm the living. The coffin also served the same purpose—double indemnity.

Q: I'm curious about the term "graveyard shift." It's very popular in factories up north. Did it start there?

Julie Bunker
Lewisville, TX

A: The *graveyard shift* means the most ghostly hours of employment. Although a popular term during World War II in northern factories, it actually started among Texas cowboys and was used to designate the lonely watches of trail-herd guards who circled the herd from midnight until first light.

Even before moving north, the term was popular in Texas hospitals where a common notion was that patients who die generally select the hours between midnight and dawn.

Q: While I was in London, I frequently heard the natives' quaint expression the loo *for the water closet. How did it originate?*

Mrs. J. W. Glover
Midland, TX

A: Like many pretty words, it is of French origin. It comes from *lieux d'aisances,* which translates *places of convenience*—another term for what in the Texas outback is known as the outhouse.

Q: I'm confused about the words larrupin' *and* larruping. *When reading about sports heroes of the past, we note that Lou Gehrig was called "Larrupin' Lou" and Max Baer was billed as the "Livermore Larruper." Yet when I visit Texas I hear the word* larruping *frequently used in the meaning of something superior, something that tastes good. Is there any relationship between the two words?*

Robert Trezevant
Oak Park, IL

A: It's the same word only with different meanings, according to our informants. Lee Kanner, sports editor of *The New York Times,* writes:

"Lou Gehrig was called Larrupin' Lou. He was so nicknamed by a long-forgotten sports writer fond of alliteration. Since *larrup* means to thrash, flog, or beat, and Gehrig was a great hitter or flogger of a baseball, the nickname came easily to the sports writer. It also, in a day of extravagant sports writing, made good copy. I do hope this helps."

Bert Sugar, editor of *Ring Magazine,* reported on Baer:

"Max was probably the deadliest righthand hitter in boxing. But he avoided infighting and threw his punches from afar, sometimes in a flailing motion. Since he picked up his mail in Livermore, California, the 'Livermore Larruper' was a natural development in an age that was crazy over alliteration."

The adjective *larruping* is defined in the *English Dialect Dictionary* as "thumping, whopping, expressive of unusual size," and this meaning came to connote more, something unusually good, especially something unusually good to the taste, the meaning you heard in Texas. For example, that meaning is the one the late author Frank X. Tolbert sometimes assigned to a well prepared "bowl of red"—chili.

The process is called semantic change; words change and their meanings change.

Q: Upon hearing one of my problems, my friend ruefully shook her head and said: "That's a doozy." Then we both started laughing. What in the world is a "doozy," and how did the expression get started?

Kristin Gazley
Dallas, TX

A: A *doozy* is anything outstanding of its kind. There are two explanations for its origin, one popular and one scholarly.

Folk etymologists and used-car salesmen maintain that it revolves around the elegant Duesenberg automobile of 1928, Model J. According to the *Encyclopedia of Motor Cars,* it "was the most remarkable automobile in America: bigger, faster, more elaborate and more expensive than any other, yet also superior to them in refinement and good looks . . . capable of 116 mph in top gear and 89 mph in second . . . weighing more than 4,980 pounds." Nicknamed the *Doozy,* it sold for $40,000—in 1928.

It was natural then that the term *doozy* would be transferred to anything else that was remarkable, distinct, and expensive, such as your problem.

So much for the popular explanation.

On the other hand, scholars point out (our source is Dr. Charles Linck, president of the Texas Folklore Society) that long before Charles and August Duesenberg began manufacturing luxury cars, the term *doozy* was being applied to things outstanding and unique, especially in the rural areas of West Virginia, eastern Ohio, and Nebraska. Hard evidence is lacking, but Professor Linck theorizes that *doozy* is an alteration of *daisy,* which has meant something "unique and outstanding" in both England

and America since the 18th century. Followers of *Little Lord Fauntleroy* may recall the sentence "She's the daisiest girl I ever saw, well, she's just a daisy, that's what she is." Duesenberg's *doozy* possibly reinforced a trend.

Even today, "a first-rate person or thing" is carried as one definition of *daisy* in *Webster's New Collegiate,* itself one doozy of a dictionary.

Q: Some seed catalogs refer to the tomato as a love apple. *I looked it up in my dictionary and all it said was that this was "archaic." Neither did the dictionary say whether the tomato is a fruit or a vegetable. Or is the jury still out on this one?*

Keith Rawlings
Greenville, TX

A: Love apple comes from the French. Since our Gallic cousins call the potato *pomme d'terre* (earth apple), it was somewhat consistent to dub the tomato *pomme d'amour* (love apple). If you don't think tomatoes can be lovable, you haven't seen those at the Folies Bergere.

One theory for the term *love apple* was that in the 16th century the tomato was considered an aphrodisiac, but this was only conjecture. From time immemorial our tomato has been associated with magical properties. The Indians of South America believed it to be a gift of Quetzacoatl, the god of healing.

According to the judges of the Supreme Court of the United States, the tomato is legally a vegetable. We're not sure if botanists will agree. Some of them tell us that the tomato belongs to the same family as poison ivy.

Q: I recently read where CBS was suing a new magazine called Digital Audio *because (CBS claimed) it caused confusion with the CBS magazine* Audio, *an older publication. I thought that words were in the public domain.*

LeShawn Hendrix
Greenville, TX

A: Actually not every word in the English language, even in a country as free as ours, is in the public domain. Some words are legally owned by individuals and companies; for example, any trademark. But to become a trademark, a term must meet certain criteria.

For example, *Playboy* was ruled a trademark in a 1980 court case because it was suggestive. Some other words that met this criterion with their second meanings were *7-Eleven* and *Hula Hoop.*

The trademark problem is more understandable when one considers some of the terms that failed to obtain trademark status because, although descriptive, they lacked secondary meaning: *Raisin-Bran, Yellow Pages,* etc.

But there is another criterion. *Coke* was granted trademark status when the courts ruled it non-generic. *Uncola, Levi's,* and *Teflon* were similarly ruled non-generic terms. On the other hand, names such as *Cola, Shredded Wheat,* and *Thermos* were denied trademark protection because they were generic.

A pharmaceutical that became a headache for its manufacturer was branded *Aspirin.* Here was a textbook case in which a brand name through popular use became generic.

Going back to the case you cite, we checked with Wayne Green, publisher of *Digital Audio,* who told us that CBS has dropped the suit.

Those interested in trademarks will find some of the technicalities discussed in the March 29, 1986 *New York Times.*

Q: As a lifelong Republican, I've always been interested in the origin of our Republican symbol, the majestic elephant.

Our two commissioners, Gary Greenough and Lambert Mims, have a similar question about the donkey and another political party, the name of which escapes me for the moment.

Can you help?

Robert B. Doyle, Jr.
Mayor of Mobile, AL

A: There are many theories, but fortunately also a few facts. One of the theories, cited in Francis Curtis' *Republican Party* was that the elephant was a natural symbol for the Republicans because of its cleverness and unwieldiness.

"He is an animal easy to control until he is aroused; but when frightened or stirred up, he becomes absolutely unmanageable. Here we have all the characteristics of the Republican." The speaker here, a politician named N.A. Elsberg, was a Republican.

As for the "other party," if we go back as far as 1844, it was referred to as the "Rooster Party" by Whigs, but four years later, *Field Piece,* a Whig newspaper, showed a donkey in a cartoon with the label "Democratic platform." But note that it did not represent the donkey as the emblem of the party. It was merely satirizing the Democratic platform.

Meanwhile, back with the G.O.P., an 1860 edition of the *Railsplitter* showed a woodcut of an elephant in elegant boots carrying a banner in his trunk with the words, "We are coming." The occasion was a demonstration for Abraham Lincoln.

But these were isolated instances. Very few people identified the two parties with their current symbols; it took a series of cartoons by Thomas Nast in *Harper's Weekly* to do that around 1874.

Strangely enough, in the first of these cartoons, the donkey did not represent the Democratic Party but the *New York Herald,* and the elephant did not symbolize the G.O.P., but merely the Republican vote. It seems that the *Herald* had been carrying on a long campaign against President Grant and the prospect of a third term. A Nast cartoon in *Harper's Weekly* showed a donkey (the *Herald*) wearing a lion's skin who was frightening away all the other animals in the forest including the elephant (the Republican vote).

Other cartoonists picked up the symbols. Following the rhetorical device of *synecdoche* (the part for the whole), they identified the elephant as the Republican party rather than the Republican vote. The donkey made a similar transition.

With these two beasts, Nast encapsulated the difference between the two major parties, " . . . the slightly ridiculous but tough and long-lived donkey—the perfect symbol of the rowdy Democrats," (we are quoting Clinton Rossiter) "the majestic but ponderous elephant—the perfect symbol of respectable Republicans. Can anyone imagine the donkey as a Republican and the Elephant as a Democrat?"

Q: I have two queries:
(1) What is the origin of the term Indian summer? *Someone told me that Indian summer can only begin after the first frost.*
(2) Why do we call a spade a Bill Dukey?

Paula Weaver
Pancake, TX

A: Your informant was correct. Indian summer cannot start until we have had a frost. Back in colonial times, when the first settlers began pulling up their plants after the first light frost, their neighbors advised them just to cover the plants and not pull them because "summer will come again." The settlers then called this period *Indian summer* out of gratitude to their benefactors. Their neighbors were Indians.

Perhaps it is a teleological exercise, but nature seems to consistently provide a pleasant twilight before darkness. Patients with optical problems have reported that their vision approached 20-20 just before they were afflicted with cataracts.

In Juliet's tomb, Romeo observed:

How oft when men are at the point of death
Have they been merry! which their keepers call
A lightning before death. . .

Indian summer is nature's granting an ameliorating reprieve before slapping you with a hard winter.

As to your question about the *Bill Dukey*, at least 10 people have submitted this same query. Two hardware suppliers, True Temper in Shirestown, Pennsylvania and Ames in Parkersburg, West Virginia, did not know. We even wrote to a Dukey family in Chicago, but that clan turned out to be made up of musicians.

* * *

Calling a spade a *bill dukey* generated many responses from readers who dig the mysteries of word origins. A few follow:

Bill Payne of Dallas:

"Here is my theory, with no proof, based on my experiences and observations.

"The few of us remaining who have used a variety of hand tools know that many of them are commonly called names, usually not found in a dictionary, that are derived from the functions or shapes of the tools. Examples: *snow, stable,* or *grain* shovels; *rat-tail* files; *garden* and *duck-bill* spades.

"A two-or three-year-old child watches its father using a duck-bill to dig a deep, narrow ditch. The child asks, 'Daddy, what are you doing?' He replies, 'I'm using a duck-bill.' The child tries, but can't say *duck-bill* and finally changes the term to *bill dukey.* The parents adopt the term and repeat it to neighbors, and finally it becomes generally accepted by many users . . ."

L.B. McKinley of Dallas:

". . . The blade of such a spade is long and narrow, with a slightly rounded body and rounded tip, much like the bill of a duck, unlike the shape of the conventional shovel.

"I can imagine a person turning to his fellow workman and asking to be handed the *duck bill,* this in turn became *bill ducky,* then later the easier to pronounce or slurred *bill dukey.* "

Temple Nash of Kaufman, Texas:

"I seem to recall having read somewhere many years ago that the type of trenching shovel we call *sharpshooter* or *bill dukey* was originally used in France and was given the French name (if my spelling is correct) of *beldeuque* which was changed to *bill dukey* by ditch diggers in this country . . ."

Roger K. Harlan of Dallas:

"*Bill Dukey—Bill Dookee—Bilduque.*

"I think we are indebted to our Mexican workmen for the name of this tool, if not the tool itself. It is not merely a spade, but a very special one with a sturdy wooden handle and a narrow, long blade of strong steel that almost can't be broken with the most furious use. Attached to a stout wooden staff some six to eight feet long it would resemble a Spanish *bilduque,* a weapon seen in earlier days around thrones, palaces, or in the hands of noblemen in battles. Don't the Papal Swiss Guards carry something of the sort?

"Whether the word is combipruning hook and battle weapon used by peasantry, combined with *duque* in its Continental guard duty application in defense of or use by nobility is something I believe can be established by the research I haven't time for."

Diane Cook of Dallas:

". . . The word is just one more of the many we absorbed from Spanish so long ago that the origins have been forgotten by most speakers of English. You can find *belduque* in Merriam-Webster's *New International Dictionary.* At least my Second Edition has it. It is defined as a 'narrow sheath knife.' The usage is Southwestern United States and it is supposed to have come through Mexican Spanish from the Spanish word *verdugo,* which they define as a kind of sword.

"The *Diccionario de la Academia Real* of the Royal Spanish Academy defines *belduque* as a large knife with a pointed blade and says that, because of the source of these knives, the word comes from the same origin as *balduque,* the Spanish word for "red tape." According to the Royal Academy dictionary, *balduque* was from *Bolduque,* which the Spanish called the city of *Bois-le-Duc* in Holland, where such narrow red ribbon (and presumably pointed knives) was made.

"A *Bill Dukie* (sic) was always a staple item around our house. My father, the late Dr. John A. Cook, was an enthusiastic gardener and practiced wielder of *Bill Dukies,* which he sometimes referred to as *sharpshooters.* He was also a native Texan and chairman of the Spanish department at Southern Methodist University. I got my original education on the subjects of both *Bill Dukies* and Spanish from him. I'm afraid I never learned to use the *Bill Dukie* as he did, but I do teach Spanish at Highland Park High School."

Q: What is a notch as in the term notch babies? If notch is an acronym, what does it stand for?

Elsie Bechtel
Alice, TX

A: Notch is a term that originated in the Washington office of the Social Security Administration and refers to a person or group of persons adversely affected by a particular Social Security regulation. It is not an acronym. It is basic governmentese that seems to have sprung as spontaneously from office memos as did *zilch.*

The semantic meanderings of *notch* demonstrate how a general term can become narrowly specific. Just as there are many poets in the world but only Shakespeare is referred to as *The Poet,* so in the bureaucratic bastion of Social Security there are many notches but only one designated as *The Notch.*

The Notch encompasses victims of legislation passed in 1977. In an effort to correct incongruities in the Social Security System, Congress passed a bill that year that—although well intentioned—discriminated against citizens born between January 1, 1917, and December 31, 1921.

Since we are talking about a million Americans who could lose up to $175 a month, this particular notch has become known as *The Notch.* The citizens caught in *The Notch* are known in Social Security waiting rooms as *notch babies.*

XI.

BI#

Literature:
Where can I find
this passage?

Q: The English language is considered by many to be the most expressive of all languages. Certainly much of the world's finest literature has been written in English. Which leads me to my question: What are the oldest extant writings in English? Who wrote it? Where is it kept? Are reproductions available?

Gordon Babbitt
Red Oak, TX

A: Most of the remains of the earliest written English, dating back to the 7th century, are poetic. And most are solemnly religious. An exception is this lament of a young girl torn between passion for her lover and duty to her husband. Her lover's name is Wulf and her husband's name is Eadwacer. We don't know her name, but her torchy song goes:

> Oh, Wulf, my Wulf, it was my longing after thee
> That made me sick.
> Dost thou hear, Eadwacer?

At this point, the reader realizes that Eadwacer is the name of her husband. His name is straight from the establishment.

> I waited for my Wulf with far wandering longings
> When it was rainy weather and I sat tearful.
> When the brave warrior clasped me in his arms,
> It was joy to me, yet it was also pain.
> Oh Wulf, my Wulf . . . .

This anonymous *Wulf and Eadwacer* (along with six other lyrics) is considered the first example of lyrical poetry in the English language.

The nameless girl wasn't the first poet in English, however. The honor of composing the first (extant) poem whose authorship is known goes to Caedmon, an illiterate farmhand from Yorkshire who is said to have been transformed by a religious experience.

Oxford's Bodleian Library probably won't check out *Hymn* to you, but any Anglo-Saxon textbook will give you an example of the reproductions. As you examine the grammar, you will note that the language is closer to German than to modern English. That's understandable: we're talking about a period seven centuries before the *Canterbury Tales.*

Q: What was the Holy Grail all about? Did anybody ever find it?

Nancy A. Winkle
Winnsboro, TX

A: The Grail was the cup used by Christ at the Last Supper and which later caught some of the precious blood at the Crucifixion. According to the legend, it was taken to Glastonbury, England, by Joseph of Arimathea where it disappeared. Eventually, (around 1200), it became the center of a tradition of Christian mysticism and also the object of search on the part of the knights of King Arthur.

Since only "the pure of heart could see God," the prize was virtually unattainable, and the impossible dream, the unattainable quest inspired hundreds of poems, thousands of lines. Every one of the 150 knights came close to seeing it, but only one found it. Sir Galahad, the kinsman of Persaval and the son of Launcelot, achieved it, and then poetically expired. This death of Galahad was one reason for the downfall of the Round Table; the other, the sinful love of Launcelot and Guinevere.

There are various explanations for the continued popularity of the Grail legend. Theologians will answer by quoting Augustine: "Thou hast made us like unto Thyself, O Lord, and our hearts will never rest until they rest in Thee." Literary critics will point out that every man is an incorrigible romantic in search of the snows of yesteryear. Movie moguls (specifically the architects of *Camelot*) tell us that it pays well at the box office. "There are always square meals at the Round Table."

Q: Last week after choir practice, we got to talking about the expression "Let me make the songs of a country and I care not who makes the laws." Our pastor said that it came from Shakespeare while the choir director argued for Sir Walter Scott. I'm sure, however, that Daniel O'Connell made this famous; and it's not just because I'm partial to Irish tenors.
Dr. Joe Nichols
Atlanta, TX

A: We too would have voted for O'Connell, but our research shows that the first person to say this was not a lyrical Irishman but a dour Scotsman, Andrew Fletcher of Saltoun (1655–1716). After championing nationalism for Scotland and murdering an occasional colleague in the process, he retired from politics and devoted his golden years to organic gardening and development of farm equipment.

As to Sir Walter Scott, he once said that without good music the digestion will suffer. Shakespeare said that music had the charm to soothe the savage breast. Shakespeare was profoundly influenced by music, and, whenever he tried to express the inexpressible, laid down his pen and called for music. The reunion scene between Lear and Cordelia is a case in point.

In the introduction to an old song called "Let Me Sing and I'm Happy," Al Jolson used to warble: "I care not who makes the laws of a nation . . ."

But if the members of your choir are interested in what great authors have said about music, the most poignant came from Nietzsche: "Without music, life would be a mistake."

Q: For years I've been intrigued by and curious about the expression "hoist with his own petard." Contextually, it's perfectly clear that it means someone caught in his own trap, but I've often wondered if I understood it clearly. Perhaps for the first time, I found it in print in Colleen McCullough's best seller An Indecent Obsession.

While hoist *is not an uncommon word, I had to consult the dictionary for* petard, *finding it to be "a case containing an explosive to be detonated—a kind of firecracker." It has almost a Shakespearean ring to it, but whoever and however was one hoisted with his own?*

Inquisitively yours,

Mrs. Elmer Wheeler
Dallas, TX

A: In days of old when chivalry was an abstract noun and castle walls a concrete reality, a knight might breach an enemy castle by placing a petard, an explosive charge, next to the wall. When successful, the hero would win fame, fortune, the king's daughter and a PFC stripe.

But the enemy wasn't always cooperative. On occasions the knight might be downed by a bolt before he could affix the charge. The smoking petard might then blow skyward the unlucky knight.

As more sophisticated methods of murder developed with the Enlightenment, the word *petard* gradually dropped out of use and probably would have disappeared entirely if it had not been immortalized earlier by the playwright you mentioned. In the third act of *Hamlet,* we find: "Tis the sport to have the engineer hoist with his own petard."

The expression is still used today to describe a person ruined by the schemes he plotted to ensnare another, a situation which rhetoricians call *tragic irony.*

Q: After reading William Humphrey's Hostages of Fortune, *I looked up* hostage *in* Webster's *and found the following: ". . . give hostages to fortune, to get, be responsible for the care of, or be liable to lose, a wife, children, etc." Please explain this idiom.*

Becky Bain
Dallas, TX

A: It's a literary allusion going back to the 17th century. Francis Bacon begins his essay "Marriage and the Single State" with the sentence "He that hath wife and children hath given hostage to fortune; for they are impediments to great enterprises, either of virtue or mischief."

Like all aphorisms this nugget of wisdom is but a half truth. Johann Sebastian Bach fathered 20 children and still managed to compose some monumental music in his spare time. The best known of all Pharoahs, Rameses II, kept his country in peace for 67 years while siring 111 sons and 50 daughters. And he was left-handed.

Q: My father often has quoted lines from a mysterious poem and neither he nor I can locate the title or the poet. I would like to know the poet, the title, or where I can find such information as well as the remainder of the poem.

> In words, like fashion, the same rule will hold,
> Alike fantastic if too new or old,
> Be not the first by whom the new is tried,
> Nor yet the last to lay the old aside.

Kurt House,
Dallas, TX

A: You and your father are to be congratulated for your retentive memories. You hit it word for word. Also we laud you for your choice of poets; Alexander Pope was one of the greatest. He is quoted so much that many of his expressions (*A little learning is a dangerous thing* . . . *Fools rush in* . . .) have passed over into the realm of cliches. Some say that he is the most often quoted author in the language, after Shakespeare and the Bible.

The work you cite is *Essay on Criticism*, Part II, line 133. You can find the poem in any library or in almost every anthology of 18th century literature.

Q: "How do I love thee? Let me count the ways . . ." is a sonnet from the Portuguese. My question is: did Elizabeth Barrett Browning write her

sonnet originally in this other language or did she simply translate the
work of a Portuguese sonneteer?

Jean Nauert
San Antonio, TX

A: Neither. She wrote her sonnets directly in English. Prior to meeting
Robert Browning, Elizabeth Barrett had been confined to a couch by the
ravages of disease and the dictates of a despotic father. Eventually she
recovered her health, partially because of a favorable climate change but
mostly because of another salubrious ingredient—true romance.

During her courtship she recorded these emotions in sonnet form, and
after her marriage when she showed them to her husband he exclaimed,
"I dare not reserve to myself the finest sonnets written in any language
since Shakespeare." The plan was to leak them to the press under the veil
of translation; and the language of the Iberian peninsula was chosen
because according to Professor Brenda Bell, "my little Portuguese" was
the first pet name he ever gave her.

Every one of us has had certain moments of sudden uplift, moments
when we walk on air and talk with God. But they are only moments. What
distinguishes the poet from the average mortal is that he can transform
the evanescent moment into a lasting monument.

Q: During an election year or during any upheaval in the Kennedy clan,
reference librarians receive questions about a passage immortalized by
Robert Kennedy: Some men see things as they are and ask, 'why?' I dream
things that never were and ask, 'why not?'
Is that original or did Kennedy get that from another source? I've heard
that he always evaded the question.

Alvin Bailey
Sherman, TX

A: Kennedy was paraphrasing George Bernard Shaw's *Back to Methuse-*
lah: You see things; and you say 'why?' But I dream things that never were;
and I say 'why not?'
It is understandable why Robert Kennedy might sidestep the question
as to the exact source. The locale in question was the Garden of Eden,
the Biblical version of Camelot; but the speaker wasn't the angel Gabriel
but the serpent.

Q: Last week when we were discussing the poem "Ulysses" by Alfred Lord
Tennyson, the name of Muhammad Ali managed to surface. Ulysses is

old; and he knows it. His strength has waned; and he knows it—a strength "which in the old days moved heaven and earth." Yet he still comes out of retirement because he believes that "some work of noble note may yet be done."

From the enthusiasm of the class discussion, I could tell that we were touching upon some universal theme. My question is where else in literature does this theme occur? Or am I asking why we love the past so much?

Sidney Hicks
Farmersville, TX

A: We truly love the past because we know how it came out: the wars are done; the loves are consummated. And literature is filled with examples.

Byron's prisoner of Chillon had "learned to love despair." and resisted liberation from "his second home" because . . . "my very chains and I grew friends." Ali also was a prisoner of the past: 26 of his first 38 years were tied up with boxing.

The simple fact is that we seek the familiar, and the more familiar we are with the familiar, the more we seek it. Marriage may be a case in point. ". . . Marriage is often more interesting and infinitely more significant than a passionate romance (we are quoting Goethe) even when that marriage is very unhappy." And should the victim divorce this partner, the victim, as we've all seen, will often re-marry the same partner (mostly different in name only) for we all seem to learn to love our familiar chains.

Now while Byron and Goethe explain Ali's fatal fascination with his past, that doesn't explain our fascination with Ali. Why do we care?

We care about Ali because he is a hero and the return of a hero always elicits certain psychological responses. In all cultures, even those separated by time and space, there has grown up a prodigal-son motif, some theme about the return of the native which literary critics have labeled as "hero archetypes." The hero is separated; the hero is transformed; and then he returns.

How many movie marshals, after retirement, strap on their guns to save the town in just one more shootout?

Look how Beowulf came out of retirement to fight the dragon. Look how Hamlet is transformed after his sea voyage and escape from the pirates. It doesn't matter that dragons never existed or that the Pirates often have second-division seasons; we are celebrating the return of the hero.

One final note: though the chains of Ali may be heavy, at least they have been plated with gold, annealed in organically grown karat juice, and retail for about nine million bucks.

* * *

Our comparison of the return to the ring by Muhammad Ali and the return to "noble work" of Alfred Lord Tennyson's aging Ulysses (a love for the past and the familiar) brought this comment by Ernestine P. Sewell of the University of Texas at Arlington's Department of English:

"Isn't there another explanation for our response to the Ulysses-Ali exit from middle-class management roles into more challenging, physical, speculative, and primitive activity?

"Old folks' retirement villages loom large upon our perceptions these days. To avert the future we perceive, and as a hangover from the recent counter-culture awareness, we entertain in several popular songs the strong suggestion to leave the conventional, comfortable, suburban home, wife, family, position, and hit the open road. Inflation and recession reinforce the urge. If only we had the requisite nerve!

"Youth sees all this. Youth seeks adventure; civilized safety is no challenge. Gloria Steinem cites the little girl child who says if she were a *boy,* she could 'fly over the city.' Youth dares to do dangerous things to avoid the humdrum of tiresome comfort, admires the wish to put off retirement as long as can be.

"The Ulysses-Ali rejection, in awe-inspiring fashion, the rejection I say of fading away like old soldiers, is the cause of our enthusiastic response, is it not?"

Q: Could you help me find a poem? Here is what I remember of it: "God and the soldier we all adore . . ."

Dianne Saucier
Dallas, TX

A: Here is the poem, "God and the Soldier."

God and the soldier
All men adore,
In time of trouble
And no more;
For when war is over
And all things righted,
God is neglected—
The old soldier slighted.

This was said to have been found in an old stone sentry box at Gibraltar. Sometimes the lines have been adapted to read "God and the doctor . . ."

We were unable to find even a guess at the author's name. But the little poem dates back centuries to a time when there was a passion for anonymity, long before ASCAP.

Q: What is the difference between blank verse and free verse, if any?

Mary Ann Palasotti
Roxton, TX

A: Blank verse is unrhymed iambic pentameter. In each line there are 10 syllables with the accent on syllable numbers two, four, six, eight, and ten. Each bar contains two syllables.

(1)The (2)cur/(3)few (4)tolls/ (5)the (6)knell/(7)of (8)part/(9)ing(10)day.

At one time, it was the most popular verse form in English. Surrey used it in the Aeneid, Milton in *Paradise Lost,* and Shakespeare in all his dramas.

Although superseded today by anapest (two unaccented syllables followed by an accented one), unrhymed iambic pentameter was once the most natural meter to talk with. But Shakespeare had plenty of company. Blank verse was also the favorite meter of the Romantics who distrusted not only restraint, but also reason and rhyme.

Free verse goes one better. For while blank verse still has regular meter and regular stress, *vers libre* is basically cadenced prose arranged in sections resembling stanzas or verse.

Walt Whitman introduced it into the United States, but its history goes way back. We see traces of it in *Canticle of Canticles* and certainly in Milton's *Lycidas.*

Free verse hasn't always had a good press. Traditionalists say it is like playing tennis without a net, yet it remains the most popular verse form today, possibly because it reflects the fragmentation of today's society (as distinct from the orderly world of the Renaissance), possibly because the modern poet feels he should convey his thought unhampered by structure or form.

Q: Within hours after the shuttle disaster in late January, President Reagan said something to the effect that the astronauts had "reached for the stars and touched the face of God." Was this a quotation? If so, could you tell me the source?

Lee A. Gilman
Dallas, TX

A: Your paraphrase was fairly accurate. The exact quotation from the president was ". . . and slipped the surly bonds of Earth (to) touch the face of God." It is from the poem "High Flight." The author was John Gillespie Magee, an American volunteer with the Royal Canadian Air Force who was killed in training in 1941.

Q: My Mom spoke of her Dad quoting "My poor Dog Trey" to her when she was a girl. He was of Irish descent. She is unaware of the author. Any ideas?

Anna Vasicek
Plano, TX

A: If he's the same dog, it's from a song. The chorus, in one version, goes:

> Old Dog Tray ever faithful
> Grief cannot drive him away;
> He is gentle, he is kind
> I'll never never find
> A better dog than Old Dog Tray.

The song was written in 1855 by Stephen Collins Foster (1826–1864), a musician who sat around Pittsburgh and wrote lovely songs about the South: "Swanee River," "Oh, Susanna," "Camptown Races," "Jeanie With the Light Brown Hair," "Beautiful Dreamer," and many more.

Why he selected the name *Tray,* we don't know, but maybe a reader will. A 1940s movie about Foster glossed over his last days as a Bowery bum in New York and his death in Bellevue Hospital. The movie starred Al Jolson and Don Ameche, the well-known break dancer.

Q: It has been said that President Reagan is the first president since Lincoln to have a genuine gift for language. Has anyone examined his speeches and the reason for their success?

Monti A. Renner
Greenville, TX

A: There have been several studies. Most of them attribute the success of Reagan's speeches to the happy relationship that exists between the President and his speech writers. Reagan is particularly fond of the work of one writer of Irish ancestry.

The standard procedure is for a writer to make a draft of a speech and then circulate it among the policy-makers and certain members of the cabinet. Each of these then will adjust the tone and wording to conform to preconceived policy. Only then will the final draft be submitted to the president.

But when Peg Noonan, a comely colleen with a flair for words, writes a speech, the originals are said to go untouched all the way to the president. Why? Because he likes the way they sound.

To quote *Esquire* (December 1985):

"The 34-year-old speech writer and the 74-year-old president are on the same wave length. They are both true believers and Noonan has done the draft for some of the president's most *true-believer* speeches."

They are also both steeped in Irish lore, the mysticism of Yeats and the lyricism of O'Casey.

Both Reagan and Noonan are consummate artists with words. They also share the same world-vision, the same telepathic wave-length. It took the writer just minutes to create the president's monumental message at the Normandy landing commemoration and reportedly even less time to achieve a brief message of transcendence immediately after the shuttle disaster in January.

Q: As a native of England, I find many words in Rockwall County different from those in London and its suburbs. In every case, my fellow students (I'm a senior in high school) have helped me, except with one. What is a gipper? *It rhymes with* kipper. *And why does one want to "win one for the gipper"?*

Melanie Parker
Rockwall, TX

A: George Gipp, a backfield star at Notre Dame, was voted the football player of the year in 1920. But if success was sweet, it was also short-lived. To quote from *Rockne to Parseghian*, "The season had hardly ended when he became desperately ill and the nation watched his losing fight through daily bulletins. There was no penicillin then and the snows of Christmas powdered the grave of Thanksgiving's hero." Eight years later,

Knute Rockne, the Notre Dame coach, tried to turn the tragedy of George Gipp into a triumph when he invoked Gipp's memory to inspire an injury-riddled Irish eleven against Army, a 4-to-1 favorite. Rockne told his team:

"The day before he died, George Gipp asked me to wait until the situation seemed hopeless—and then ask a Notre Dame team to go out and beat the Army for him. This is the day and you are the team."

Notre Dame did win, in a come-from-behind 12-to-6 upset. And "win one for the Gipper" became a battle cry and a legend. It became even more popular in 1940 with the Warner Brothers' film *Knute Rockne, All-American,* and took on new relevance in 1980 when the actor who played the Gipper became president of the United States.

XII.

The Writer

Q: What would you advise to be the best background for a writer? My friends often turn up in the strangest places and tell me they are gathering material for a novel. Is it true that most novelists do and should write from experience?

Cliff Vlasik
Victoria, TX

A: Great writers aren't spawned in ivory towers. Whether bricklayers like Ben Jonson, plowboys like Robert Burns, or denizens of the gutter like Francois Villon, the greatest writers came into close contact with life and reality. Some experienced life at the top. Dante Alighieri was an envoy, Geoffrey Chaucer an ambassador, and Johann Wolfgang von Goethe a prime minister.

Even with the Romantic writers, poetry was only an avocation. Current events of their day consumed most of them much of the time.

Your friends may reason that it's logical for them to study life at its earthiest. Walks on the wild side have produced some fine novels. But all of us occasionally must wonder why the dregs of society are so often considered the ultimate repository of wisdom.

On one point, however, we have no doubt, and that is the first requirement for a writer—a love affair. A writer must fall in love with language. He must love words for their own sake, for their power and beauty, and especially for the wonderful things he can do with them.

If experience alone produced writers, then all our novels would be written by sheriff's deputies, surgical nurses, and managers of massage parlors.

The importance of experience to a novelist can, of course, be overstated. Edgar Rice Burroughs didn't swing on vines and Lewis Carroll seldom conversed with rabbits.

The realistic writer must embrace life. But he must love words.

In the beginning was the word. It still is.

Q: Whenever the question of correctional institutions fulfilling their function comes up, we are given the list of inmates who have been successfully rehabilitated while references are made to great books that have been written in prison. But no one ever tells us what these books are.

This seems like a question for your column.

Lee Clark
Attorney at Law
Greenville, TX

A: There's no end of significant works written in prison. In fact, they include some of the greatest. And there's a reason, if we are to believe Don King, the boxing promoter: "A person can think better if he's a little hungry and meditate better when it's freezin' ass cold. And if you just happen to be in jail, it's surprising how much better you can write and how much longer you can study. I came out armed with knowledge."

In the *Sixteen Books That Changed the World,* Robert Downs has *The Prince* of Niccolo Machiavelli as number one. It influenced Charles the Fifth, Frederick the Great, Cromwell, Bismarck, Napoleon, and Henry the Fourth, who was carrying a copy with him at the time he was murdered. Yet *Il Principe* might never have been written if this secretary had not been tortured, imprisoned, and exiled. *The Prince* was also favorite bedtime reading of one Adolph Hitler, who did a bit of scribbling himself while awaiting trial in Landsberg. Though *Mein Kampf* is tedious and repetitive (in private conversation, Hitler apologized for its monotony, "I didn't have the guts to write what I wanted to write"), it sold more than 10 million copies and changed the course of the 20th century.

But all the tomes written in the slammer were not political tracts. There were major religious works like Bunyan's *Pilgrim's Progress* and parts of the *Bible* (like the *Revelations* of John), the ascetical work of Boethius, *Consolations of Philosophy,* and romances like *Morte D'Arthur,* in which Malory idealized both chivalry and chastity—while serving an extended term for rape. The travelogues of Marco Polo would have been lost to posterity if that indefatigable traveler had not been imprisoned in Genoa; Leigh Hunt's insulting of the Prince Regent also led to some pretty good hack work.

Then there were the poets, Richard Lovelace and Oscar Wilde. "I could not love thee, dear, so much, loved I not honor more." Even under the most unfavorable conditions, a poet can take an emotion, add a few simple words, and they will rise up like a flock of singing birds. "Yet each man kills the thing he loves" is one of the most romantic and pointed lines ever written.

The greatest single opus written in the penitentiary was undoubtedly *Don Quixote,* which brought Cervantes great fame but little money. Not so the *Pisan Cantos* of Ezra Pound, which earned him considerable money, the prestigious Bollingen Award and eventual release.

Other authors who used their talents to expedite a parole were O. Henry, who actually perfected his skills in prison; John Cleland, whose second-rate novel paid his way out of debtor's prison and, most famous of all, Eldridge Cleaver: "It wasn't until I smuggled *Soul on Ice* out of prison and got it into the hands of publishers that the attitude of the warden began to change . . . if I had been just another black man, I wouldn't have had a chance."

As to rehabilitation, Don King commented the day he left Marion Federal Prison: "Prison reform will never work until you guys start attracting a better class of people here."

Q: "Never eat at a place called Mom's" is part of a famous admonition to young writers. Where can I find the rest of it? I think the speaker was either a lawyer or a judge. As a manager of a bookstore, I get quite a few questions on advice to young writers.

Pat Bitowf
Spanish Fort, AL

A: The complete quotation is: "Never play cards with a man called Doc. Never eat at a place called Mom's. Never sleep with a woman whose troubles are worse than your own." Nelson Algren gives this advice to young writers in his book *A Walk on the Wild Side.* Algren concedes that these words of wit and wisdom are not original and that he obtained them not from a lawyer, judge, or jury, but from a philosopher-crook.

Q: The object of drama is to reflect reality, we are taught. Yet when certain words are declared off-limits, how can the playwright recapture in print the racy badinage of the real world? There's a social reason that I'm aware of, but is there any other reason?

Melody Jackson
Texarkana, TX

A: There is also an aesthetic reason. According to editor Max Perkins, four-letter words do not generate the same effect in print that they did in the bar or boudoir.

In a 1933 letter to Ernest Hemingway, Perkins wrote, "Four-letter words have a suggestive power for the reader which is quite often other than that which they have to those who utter them; and therefore they are not right artistically. Words should have exactly the same meaning and implication which they have when uttered."

It is possible also that you put your finger on the answer with your choice of the word *reflect.* The stage doesn't present reality, only a reflection of reality; the mission of the stage is to "hold the mirror up to nature," in the words of Shakespeare. As a playwright, he had to contend with language restrictions from both the Puritans and the Licensing Act. Nevertheless, he was able to achieve financial success while living and immortality after leaving the stage.

Q: It has been said that the reason Abraham Lincoln's Gettysburg Address was so successful and famous was that it had so few words with more than one syllable in them.

Was this because his education was so short of long, hard-to-understand words?

L.H. Ensley
Dallas, TX

A: There are many instances when a man of great lore and learning has employed simple language to construct a masterpiece.

In his lecture on Shakespeare, the journalist Lafcadio Hearn went to great pains to employ simple language because his Japanese audience had only a limited knowledge of English. He came up with an interesting lecture for his listeners and, almost as a byproduct, one of the clearest commentaries on the secret of Shakespeare's power for later readers.

Of the 100,000 words in *Paradise Lost,* only eight per cent of them have more than two syllables. *The Ancient Mariner* has about 3,000 words—only 60 of more than two syllables. "Flanders Fields" does not have one word with more than two syllables.

And no one could accuse the authors of those three poems of a poverty of vocabulary.

Likely, Lincoln had a rich vocabulary of longer words but was merely following the advice of Alexander Pope, one of the finest writers of all time:

"The great secret of how to write well is to know thoroughly what one writes about and . . . to write naturally."

Q: Years ago I borrowed a book on word derivation and, unfortunately, did not get the name of the publisher or author.

What do you use or what could you recommend my getting for this purpose?

Barbara Sims
Ft. Worth, TX

A: You're probably thinking of the old standby, *Thirty Days to a More Powerful Vocabulary* by Dr. Wilfred Funk.

A favorite device of Dr. Funk, who went far in making popular his field, was to begin with a Greek root like *anthropos* (man) and form the word *philanthropy* by combining it with another Greek root *philos* (lover) and then lead over to the antonym *misanthropy* by employing another Greek root *misos* (hatred).

He would then introduce *monogamy* via *monos* (one) and *gamos* (marriage), proceed to *bigamy* with *bi* (two), and then naturally drift into *polygamy* via *poly* (many).

In exemplary Sunday school tradition, he would show how *theology* developed out of *theos* (God) and *logos* (word or study); *theocracy*, out of *theos* (God) and *kratos* (rule).

Some of the other derivatives would include the following:

Anthropos: anthropology and anthropoid.
Poly: polyglot and polyandry.
Mono: monotheism and monologue.
Bi: bicycle and biscuspid.
Misos: misogynist and misology.
Philos: philatelist and philology.
Kratos: plutocracy and aristocracy.
Theos: apotheosis and theodicy.

If Dr. Funk's book isn't available, you might look for a new book by David Ayers, *English Words From Latin and Greek Roots*, released by the University of Arizona at Tuscon.

Most teachers of vocabulary building now supplement their textbooks with records and tapes. After all, we usually learn a language through the ear. A favorite, in this approach, is the Bergen Evans program published by VOCAB, 3071 Broad Street, Chicago, Illinois, 60608.

Q: When I was growing up in Louisville, my great hero was Muhammad Ali, not just for boxing but for his poetry. Such lyrics as "I tell you that the beast is mine and tonight he falls in nine" or "Old Archie Moore will fall in four" would send me better than Chubby Checker, Fats Domino, or William Shakespeare. Now I feel like a kid without Christmas. Marcus Anderson, my trainer, tells me that a literary society in Dallas doesn't include Ali among its poets. What gives? If Ali isn't a poet, where is poetry to be found?
Greg Page
Louisville, KY

A: Glad to hear from a great Louisville slugger.

What we're talking about here is the difference between poetry and doggerel.

Doggerel (the name is unfortunate) is any jingle, any humorous verse, or verse without emotion. And it has its place. How many school kids would have learned the calendar without "Thirty days has September, etc." And what young lover could have launched his first romance without the inspiration of "Roses are red, violets are blue, etc.?"

Without catchy lines—"Moore in four"—Ali wouldn't have made such good copy for the writers, especially since Moore *did* fall in four, giving Ali a shot at the title.

What is the difference between doggerel and poetry?

There are as many definitions of poetry as there are poets and critics. But whether you go with Gwendolyn Brooks' definition of "life distilled," or Poe's "rhythmical creation of beauty" or Wordworth's "emotion recollected in tranquility," somehow the idea of experience, beauty, or emotion will surface.

Without a single rhyme, a composition may be poetic:

> . . . Falstaff sweats to death,
> And lards the lean earth as he walks along . . .

Or every other line may rhyme:

> To see the world in a grain of sand
> And heaven in a wild flower
> Hold infinity in the palm of your hand
> And eternity in an hour.

But there will always be beauty of language and poignant experience.

And what of Ali? He will be remembered in Texas both for his poetry and his jingles: the poetry of his motion and the jingles that called attention to that motion.

Q: Who is the modern fiction writer who revises every paragraph three times? I think it is a woman. Did she ever finish anything long like a novel? I always thought writing should come "as natural as the leaves to the trees."

Jeffri Ann Bowling
Russelville, AR

A: Most good writers are good rewriters. You're probably referring to the late Margery Allingham who wrote every paragraph four times: "Once to get my meaning down, once to put in everything I left out, once to take out everything that seems unnecessary, and then the fourth time to make the whole thing sound as if I had *only just thought of it.*"

In other words, the final revision gave it life so that it would seem "as natural as the leaves to the trees." Despite her meticulous methods, Miss Allingham did manage to finish a novel here and there—about 25 of them. *The New York Times* saluted her in 1961 (the year before she died) as one of England's leading mystery writers, " . . . for the first 22 years of her writing career, Miss Allingham wrote a novel almost every year. They are considered classics in their genre . . ."

She did have the advantage of an early beginning, publishing her first novel at age 16. In fact, she began writing nine years earlier under her father's tutelage.

Your quotation is from the Romantic poet John Keats: "If poetry comes not as naturally as the leaves to the trees, it had better not come at all." But the Romantic poet and the modern novelist are saying the same thing, the same as the aphorism of the classicist Alexander Pope: "The secret of writing is to know everything about a subject and then write as naturally as possible."

True there are many "writers" who do not revise. You will meet a lot of them at cocktail parties but you seldom will encounter their work in the pages of a book.

Q: I'm trying to run down a reference to Hemingway's workmanship, something about the numerous revisions to the last page of A Farewell to Arms. How many times did he revise that page and where can I find the reference?

Dr. Marck Gibson
First Baptist Church
Wolfe City, TX

A: Thirty-nine times. You can find this verification in *Writers at Work: Second Series,* edited by George Plimpton, page 222 and also in *The Making of Farewell to Arms* by M.S. Reynolds, page 49.

Q: Gary Hart has just written his fifth novel. Isn't it unusual for a politician, an administrator, also to have literary talents? They seem mutually exclusive. Or has this happened before?

Cliff Avery
Fort Worth, TX

A: Where do we begin? With the mayor of New York, a British prime minister, a vice-president of the United States, maybe even the Pope? During the Gay Nineties, Winston Churchill composed *Savrola,* a very $ucce$$ful novel. But he was not the first prime minister to publish fiction; Benjamin Disraeli had already written thirteen novels, readable and reputable enough to win him a place in the history of English literature.

During the Roaring Twenties, Jimmy Walker was a successful lyricist on New York's Tin Pan Alley before taking over the duties of mayor of that city. At the same time, a kindred spirit was writing the music for "It's All In the Game," Charles Dawes, the vice-president under Calvin Coolidge. Another budding tunesmith was also the Kingfish; the fight songs for L.S.U. were written by none other than Governor Huey Long. Who would have thought that dictators would have a flair for music and poetry?

But they do. Mao Tse-tung composed poetry during his historic Long March to north China: Adolph Hitler wrote *Mein Kampf* during his historic incarceration in southern Germany; Benito Mussolini, a historic procrastinator, actually finished a novel, *The Cardinal's Mistress,* before coming to power. Anwar Sadat, a non-dictator, also finished a novel (*The Prince of the Island*), but never got around to publishing it.

Then there were the generals: Lew Wallace (the novel *Ben Hur*), Blackjack Pershing (the Pulitzer Prize in history). And some commentators who wrote novels: Harry Reasoner (*Tell Me About Women*)—which didn't have a ghost of a chance—and Drew Pearson (*The Senator*)—which had a ghost for co-author.

Show people who published novels are Sterling Hayden (*Voyage*), Sarah Bernhardt (*In the Clouds*), Evelyn Keys (*I Am A Billboard*), and, believe it or not, Jean Harlow (*Today Is Tonight*).

Then there was the music to *The Honeymooners* by Jackie Gleason, the novel *Alpaca* by Dallasite H. Lamar Hunt, and the drama *Jeweler Shop* by John Paul the Second, poet and pontiff.

It is fitting that the first novel to fall within this syndrome was also the most significant, because it set the thought pattern for many politicians of the future.

This particular prime minister of England (Thomas More) called his work—*Utopia!*

Q: Why does the English language contain so many expressions that are slanted against left-handers? Isn't it true that left-handers can outperform right-handers in certain professions, especially those that require creativity?

Al Oliver
Arlington, TX

A: There is discrimination against left-handers because 90 percent of the population is right-handed; and you know what happens to minorities. This discrimination began a long time ago, and, as you have implied, it is metabolized into use through our language. "You can do that with your left hand," a child is told when being cajoled into performing a simple task. Song writers lump "outlaws with southpaws," and writers of etiquette advise against left-handed compliments. Neither is this discrimination limited to the English language; in ancient Latin the adjective *sinister* meant *depraved* or—*left-handed.*

But even though left-handers enter this world with two strikes against them, they are more successful in baseball than those who bat from the right side of the plate, according to the *Lefty Survival Manual,* and also outperform right-handers in such physical activities as bowling, pingpong, typing, and playing the piano.

One theory for their superiority in these spheres is that, forced to survive in a world of right-handed ice-cream scoops and can-openers, they have developed the same dexterity in the right mitt as in the left. Joseph L. Barrow, a converted southpaw, was the only boxer in history who could KO an opponent with a 6-inch jab. In 1937 he won the heavyweight championship of the world under the pseudonym of Joe Louis.

But left-handers have achieved prominence, even preeminence, in fields other than physical, as demonstrated by the political prowess of James A. Garfield, Harry S. Truman, Gerald Ford, and the artistic success of Michaelangelo, Leonardo Di Vinci, Cole Porter, and Harpo Marx. Other creative port-siders include comedians like Charlie Chaplin, sex-symbols like Betty Grable, and award-winning teachers like Tommy Ben Johnson.

The reason left-handers do so well artistically goes back to the twofold division of the brain. As is well known, the left side of the brain for right-handers thinks in words and numbers while the right side is oriented artistically. With some left-handers, but not all, the brain is a reverse image. But 50 percent of the left-handed population is bi-lateral. In other words, they use all of their brains. This gives them two advantages, according to psychologists. First, they can think analytically and holistically at the same time; second, should they ever suffer partial brain damage, they probably wouldn't lose total power of speech.

Subsequent research will tell us more about lefties.

Research will also tell us that the batting champion for the National League in 1982 was an artistic left-handed first baseman for the Montreal Expos who once played for the Texas Rangers—Al Oliver.

XIII. *Bill*

BARD
OF AVON
CALLING
CARD

W. SHAKESPEARE
555-0496

Shakespeare

Q: During the summer, when Dallas and Fort Worth offer Shakespeare-in-the-park attractions, we hear quite a few heated discussions on the authorship of Shakespeare's plays and even see occasional articles that question whether Shakespeare wrote Shakespeare. My question is: Who did write the plays of Shakespeare? Some of my lawyer friends say that it was Francis Bacon.

William P. Clements Jr.
Governor of Texas
Austin, TX

A: Well, Governor, there are three distinct points of view: the viewpoint of the Renaissance scholars, that of the Baconians, and finally that of William Shakespeare himself.

According to Renaissance scholars, the works of Shakespeare were written by William Shakespeare; the poet who lived in Stratford-on-Avon from 1564 to 1616. During the Bardolatry craze of the Romantic era, many poets and lawyers (especially lawyers) began to attribute authorship to Francis Bacon; but no Renaissance scholar of note ever shared that view.

In fact, most scholars are amused by the Baconian theory. They point to the large number of people who knew Shakespeare personally and who identified him with the plays and poems that bear his name. Some of these contemporaries were Gabriel Harvey, the Cambridge don; the playwrights Jonson, Greene, Webster, and Beaumont; and his fellow actors Heminge and Condell who also edited the *First Folio* of 1623. The poet Milton also wrote a rather adulatory sonnet to Shakespeare. There is not a scrap of evidence to show that any of Shakespeare's contemporaries ever mentioned Bacon as the author of the works we identify with Shakespeare.

IT WAS ALMOST 2½ centuries after the death of Shakespeare that the Baconian theory began to receive any sort of a hearing. The overly simple argument was that since Shakespeare did not have a rich academic background while Francis Bacon (essayist, statesman, and lawyer) certainly did, then Bacon must surely be the author of those monumental works.

By such reasoning we could "prove" that Lincoln's *Gettysburg Address* was authored by an unemployed Ph.D. from Harvard. We could "prove" that the 1,100 inventions "erroneously" attributed to Thomas Edison really belonged to Adolph Hitler because Edison had only three months of formal schooling while Adolph at least made it through high school.

The glory of Shakespeare is the language, but the fact that the relatively second-rate prose of Bacon's essays somehow lacked the verbal magic of Shakespeare's iambic pentameter never seemed to stem the conjecturing of Baconians. Baconians were good at anagrams. For instance, the longest word in the Shakespeare canon is *honorificabilituditatibus,* from which Baconians decoded "Hi ludi F. Baconis nati tuiti orbi" and then translated it into "These plays of Francis Bacon's offspring are preserved for the world."

But the most interesting Baconian conjecture came in 1956: "Bacon wrote Shakespeare, Milton, Spenser, Marlowe, *The Raven* of Edgar Allan Poe, and also edited the King James version of the Holy Bible."

Since nine-tenths of the Baconians have been lawyers, it was inevitable that this controversy would eventually reach a court of law and just as inevitable that the judge (Richard Tuthil of Cook County in Illinois) would hand down a verdict in favor of Bacon's authorship in a case involving $5,000 in damages.

As to Shakespeare's opinion, it is easy to discern. He didn't care. If he did, he would have seen to it that his plays and poems were printed in his lifetime under his name. The presses were there, but the possibility that at some future date his works would be attributed to Francis Bacon (or Christopher Marlowe, or Queen Elizabeth, or Anne Hathaway, or 40 other contenders) never seemed to bother him. Clearly, he didn't care. To Shakespeare, the play was the thing. After he made his fortune in London, he went home to his family. This was reality to him.

As to a solution of the current authorship controversy, Shakespeare would probably allude to a line from *Henry the Sixth:* "The first thing we do, let's kill all the lawyers." (Act IV, scene 2, line 76.)

Q: I'm an English major working my way through school. The people I work with often ask me why Shakespeare took five acts and two hours to tell the story of Romeo and Juliet. *Why didn't he just say "Boy meets girl, boy loses girl and there was trouble in the family"?*

Charles Hodgkiss
Paris, TX

A: First of all, the boy does get the girl, for Romeo and Juliet are re-united in the paradise of lovers. Shakespeare completes the formula. But to answer your question, the feelings to be expressed were so subtle that a mere formula would not convey them; so the Bard carried his audience through scenes, situations, and adventures until the exact, dramatic emotion could be reproduced, e.g. the glow of romance. The plot of *Romeo and Juliet* was centuries old when Shakespeare found it. But he was such a craftsman with words that any eloping teenagers can easily identify with the lovers.

Q: Your column on the witches of Halloween brought up a discussion about the witches in Macbeth. *Did Shakespeare believe in witches? Also, do scholars agree on what the witches really were: goddesses of destiny whom Macbeth was powerless to resist or merely symbolic representations of Macbeth's evil thoughts, sort of a visual aid?*

Janice Mumford
Dallas, TX

A: Shakespeare used the witches in *Macbeth* because they were dramatically appropriate and theatrically effective. It is they who establish the murky atmosphere in the exposition, point the direction that the play must inexorably follow. They provide the director—in the cauldron scene— with an opportunity for an imaginative staging.

True, part of their function is to symbolize the dark influences at work within the universe and also within the heart of Macbeth, but to label them as symbolic representations of Macbeth's evil thoughts would be totally inaccurate: until the weird sisters informed him, Macbeth had no idea of the treachery of Cawdor, the mobility of Birnam Wood, or Macduff's unusual entry into the world. Their prophecies are on the same level as the proddings of Cassius upon Brutus or the falsehoods of Iago upon Othello. They are fatal to the protagonist only because there is something in him that reacts dangerously to this catalyst.

To say that they were goddesses of destiny whom Macbeth was powerless to resist would be equally inaccurate: Shakespeare makes it abundantly clear—through the words of the witches—that they have no power over the free will of men. So much for what they are *not.*

Actually, the witches are nothing more than mean old women blessed with the intuitive gift of a psychic such as Bertie Catchings or a Jeanne Dixon. While the rest of us mortals view reality on a vertical plane, the TV screen of the psychics reveals a sort of horizontal dimension.

Whether Shakespeare believed in psychics, we do not know because (like Chaucer) he consistently eschewed any discussion of foreknowledge or predestination. Still less do we know whether he believed in witches. He never told us. What is important is that his audience did believe in witches and were profoundly affected by them.

Q: *So oft it chances in particular men,*
That for some vicious mole of nature in them . . .
that these men
Carrying, I say, the stamp of one defect . . .
Shall in the general censure take corruption
From that particular fault.

Hamlet I-iv.

I have always thought that these lines, immortalized in Shakespeare's own words, give us the complete pattern of all Shakespearean tragedy, and, as you know, I used these very lines at the beginning of my Hamlet *film. It has now been over 30 years, and I've often wondered if this introduction has been much help to teachers of Shakespeare. Do films help? How do you go about this in the States?*

Laurence Olivier
London, England

A: Time was when most of us taught Shakespeare by explaining it. On a good day we would take the above quotation, relate it to Aristotle ("The hero is a man of high nobility ending in destruction caused by a failing, a tragic flaw."), then tie it in with F. Scott Fitzgerald's aphorism: "Show me a hero and I'll write you a tragedy.")

At this point, some farm boy would point out that had Othello been in Hamlet's position he would have killed the king in the first scene of the first act, maybe before the first curtain, and this observation would lead to a discussion of Shakespeare's tragic picture of life: by some grim fatality Brutus just happened to have Cassius for a friend, the one person who could play upon Brutus' tragic flaw.

We admit that we did oversimplify a little, but basically this was the approach.

But gradually the profession has been shifting from Shakespeare explained to Shakespeare experienced; from learning Shakespeare mediately from books of scholars to immediately via the boards of the theater. And actors have been responsible for the change.

In 1874, just when the critics were writing Shakespeare off as a closet dramatist, the Duke of Meiningen brought forth a production of *Caesar* the like of which the world had never seen. "We are not dealing with something which is more or less superior, which one might have seen elsewhere. This is the realization of an entirely new principle . . . that the total effect of a dramatic work must be emphasized."

In retrospect, the message of the duke's production was so very simple: given half a chance a Shakespeare play will come to life on the stage. It was a company without stars; many of them were second rate actors. But they gave the play a chance and made one of the greatest contributions to theater in the entire 19th century. German critics said it was the greatest.

Enter the era of the film.

In 1944, long after Hollywood had despaired of converting Shakespeare to that medium ("Shakespeare never composed his plays in pictures," quoth the critics, "he was an artist in words."), a young British gunnery instructor—on an extended 3-day pass—produced a film of *Henry the Fifth,* one of Shakespeare's less significant history plays. It was an overnight sensation and during the ensuing years captured every possible award.

"This is by all odds the finest movie I have ever seen and one of the most enthralling and stirring Shakespeare performances I ever hope to see . . ." raved a leading critic. "The movies have produced one of their great works of art . . . the words, the poetry set loose in the gracious world of the screen, like so many uncaged birds, fully enjoy and take care of themselves."

Even today, Sir Laurence, no one has been able to encapsulate the formula for your successful filming of *Henry the Fifth.*

In a letter, you once commented that maybe "our little *Henry the Fifth* was just a happy, if very rare falling into place of not quite usual ingredients."

In a review, one illustrious critic posed the hypothesis that somehow your style matched Shakespeare's style. The simple truth is that you did discover the secret of letting a Shakespeare play work of itself ("like so many uncaged birds") in the medium of film and, in the process, demonstrated that his history plays are basically cinematic.

As the German historians laud the Meininger contribution as the greatest achievement in theater in the 19th century, it is quite possible that future historians will cite the Olivier contribution as the greatest of the 20th.

About your *Hamlet* film, you gave us more than an educational film or an essay on *Hamlet.* You bequeathed us a vision of greatness.

Q: Thanks to the Dallas Shakespeare Festival, I've become quite a lover of the Bard, especially of his beautiful language. Also the plays contain such healthy morals. It is for this reason that I wish someone would publish an edition of Shakespeare that would be suitable for children, an edition without so much of the natural language. This means that the editor must not only be capable, but also a person of great integrity.

Rev. James Garrett, pastor
University Park United Methodist Church
Dallas, TX

A: It has been done. The first person to attempt this was Dr. Thomas Bowdler, an amiable English gentleman, who in 1818 gave up his medical practice to perform intensive surgery on the literary works of Shakespeare, Gibbon, and God. The title reveals his intentions and integrity: *The Family Shakespeare in Ten Volumes; in which nothing is added to the original text; but those words and expressions are omitted which cannot with propriety be read aloud in a family.* In his preface he also called attention to the unnecessary and frivolous allusions to Scripture which "call imperiously for their erasement."

Although his prudery was never too popular with the Shakespeare critics, the work sold very well, which encouraged him to "bowdlerize" Gibbon's *Decline and Fall* and eventually the Old Testament. The verb *bowdlerize* did not enter our language until ten years after his death.

Q: With so many articles on John DeLorean, one notes how frequently he is characterized as a "tragic hero" or as a "protagonist with a tragic flaw." Now I always thought a tragic hero had to be a man of exalted virtue and that tragedy was something that died with Shakespeare or the Greeks. In your answer, would you define a tragic flaw? This is a term that the journalists are now kicking around with abandon.

Mario Ramirez
San Antonio, TX

A: The first requirement for a tragic hero is the dimension of greatness. There is no substitute for greatness. But he is not a Sunday school hero, rather an inscrutable compound of good and evil. According to Aristotle, the tragic hero should be a person "who is not eminently good or just, yet whose misfortune is brought about by some error or frailty."

This frailty is called a tragic flaw—a fault in a character which though perhaps small in itself is sufficient to cause the destruction of the hero. It is always an excess. Macbeth is *too* ambitious; Hamlet, *too* idealistic; Lear, *too* credulous; Othello loves not wisely but *too* well.

It is easy to see why commentators would dub DeLorean a tragic character. There is a reversal of fortune; he falls from a height; and the feds say he has a flaw. But is he a tragic hero? We will have to wait for the final curtain.

This isn't the first time that the press has employed the terminology of tragedy. During the Watergate scandal, President Nixon was compared to both Richard II and Richard III. In fact, it was at least partially due to Watergate coverage that *Richard II* enjoyed its most successful run since the abdication of the king of Britain in 1937.

Marshall McLuhan even spelled it out: "Richard Nixon is a tragic hero. His tragic flaw was his failure to recognize that he could not defend his own privacy while depriving others of theirs."

As to your question of whether we can have tragedy today, much of the answer depends on the answer to another question: "Has man lost his concept of greatness?"

The tragic hero knows he is being destroyed, yet he has the guts to face it. And we in the audience are touched by the invincibility of the human spirit. The result is catharsis.

Q: As an actor, I read as much literary criticism as I can, but as a bardolator, I'm always perturbed when a critic denigrates Shakespeare. Two critics have accused Shakespeare of writing a purple patch: first in the "tomorrow and tomorrow" of Macbeth; *second in the description of the barge in* Antony and Cleopatra. *I would have written those critics a nasty letter or so, but I was not sure of one item. What is a purple patch?*

Frank Wyatt
Irving, TX

A: A purple patch is a section of literary work in which the author places less emphasis on *what* is being said and more on *how* it is being said. "Watch me write," he keeps telling us in his pregnant piece of midnight imagery as he heaps polysyllable upon polysyllable upon parallelism.

Alexander Pope ridiculed purple patches in *Rape of the Lock,* while Oscar Wilde demonstrated one in *Salome* in which Herod described his treasure.

One dead giveaway of a purple patch is that it stands out from the rest of the composition. From this standpoint, one cannot fault the 10 lines of "tomorrow and tomorrow" because the other 695 lines that Macbeth speaks frequently sing with poetry. As to the description of the barge in *Antony and Cleopatra,* it comes almost word for word from Plutarch. Shakespeare knew a good speech when he saw one.

Another appellation for purple patch is euphuistic writing or writing that smells of the lamp—or midnight oil.

In art and literature, the color purple has always implied the regal and princely. The term has been around a long time: Horace used it in *Ars Poetica.*

Going back to your original observation, the late Max Reinhardt used to say that in controversies involving actor and critic he always deferred to the actor rather than to the critic, who frequently "was a creative writer who didn't make the big time or a university professor who couldn't get tenure."

Q: I was arranging my schedule so that I could attend the Shakespeare plays in Dallas when I was informed that they were doing Shakespeare Apocrypha this season. As an actor, I'm embarrassed to admit that I am woefully ignorant of Shakespeare and have no idea what the Shakespeare Apocrypha is. Could you help?

Jerry Biggs
Greenville, TX

A: To begin with, both *Hamlet* and *Midsummer Night's Dream,* the two plays you mention in your letter, belong to the Shakespeare canon and not to the Apocrypha.

But since you asked, the Shakespeare Apocrypha are the plays that are spurious, those which an unscrupulous publisher tried to foist upon the public by inscribing the name William Shakespeare upon the title page—for even in the seventeenth century the name of William Shakespeare carried a lot of clout.

The two most notorious plays in the Shakespeare Apocrypha are *Arden of Feversham* and *The Yorkshire Tragedy,* neither of which compares with the authentic thirty-seven plays in plot construction, character delineation, metrical patterns—not to mention their complete lack of universality.

The word *apocrypha* has a direct connection with the Holy Bible and was coined by St. Jerome (331–420 A.D.) to designate those pseudo-biblical books that did not belong to the canon, ascetical works like "The Life of Adam and Eve," "The Childhood of Jesus," etc., which the cognoscenti did not accept as "inspired."

Thus there is a Biblical Apocrypha, a Shakespeare Apocrypha, a Chaucer Apocrypha. There is also the adjective *apocryphal* which is frequently used today to characterize certain anecdotes about heroes like, say, George Washington or Babe Ruth: the cherry-tree episode of

Washington, the Bambino calling his shot in the '32 World Series at Wrigley Field. These are incidents that flavor the savor of this particular hero but have no foundation in reality.

Q: I'm looking for an article that treats the secret of Shakespeare's power. We had a total audience of 1,600 people when we opened in 1972; in 1980 it was 43,000. I'm aware of the process that contributed to the local success, but how about the product? What do the high priests of literary criticism say on this topic, the secret of Shakespeare's power?

Robert Glenn
Shakespeare Festival of Dallas
Dallas, TX

A: The critics would probably say that the Fair Park success revolves around the way you have introduced Shakespeare. While high schools continue to introduce William as a poet and colleges treat him as a thinker or philosopher—both with limited success—your establishment has presented him as a playwright, and the numbers speak for themselves.

It is easy to forget that, except for the sonnets, Shakespeare never wrote for the printed page and seemed to have had no interest in it whatsoever. But the organ he attacked was the human ear. To him the play was the thing, the play that came alive on the stage. When he went to his grave there was no collected edition of his plays—the presses were there, but he obviously didn't care. He had seen the play on the stage.

(One theory is that, during his active years in the theater, Shakespeare may have wished to guard his works against theft by rival troupes of players and other playwrights. Most scholars agree, however, that the Bard ignored the press because he was writing his plays for theater audiences rather than readers.)

It is no small coincidence that in the two countries where he enjoys his greatest popularity, England and Germany, it was the boards of the actor and not the books of the scholar that introduced his plays. None of the Elizabethans ever read the printed text of Shakespeare. There was none. And most of them couldn't read anyhow. But they could hear; they could feel; they could learn the aesthetic experience of drama, the catharsis of creation that results from interaction of audience and actor.

And two centuries later, it got better.

At that time, Germany consisted of a bewildering number of dukedoms. As a status symbol, every German duke or duchess maintained a court jester and a court theater. But there was an added joker: there were no German playwrights. Fortunately, the plays of Shakespeare were translated at this time, and the rest is history. Germany was soon outdistancing England in Shakespearean productions and today still produces more Shakespeare than the stages of England, the United States, and the rest of the world combined.

All he ever needed was a stage, whether it was in Duesseldorf or Dallas.

As to his exact secret, many critics address the problem; the most lucid is by Mark Van Doren:

"It is literally true that when we see a Shakespeare play we are in it. We may be drawn in swiftly or slowly—in most cases it is swiftly—but once we are there we are enclosed. That is the secret, and it is still a secret of Shakespeare's power to interest us . . . Shakespeare who denies his spectator nothing, denies him least of all the excitement of feeling that he is where things are simply and finally alive."

XIV.

Philosophy

Q: We know that there is a relationship between vocabulary and intelligence, but has anyone ever made a study of the relationship between intelligence and morality? Does knowledge lead to virtue?

Hector Arce
Harlingen, TX

A: It all depends on whom you ask.

Educators and politicians often aver that there is a direct relationship (especially when a big bond issue is at stake). They point to the generally low intelligence scores of convicts to "prove" that only people with limited intelligence (or education) stoop to crime.

On the other hand, you may freely consider, along with other factors, the possibility that only the dumbest crooks get caught and convicted.

If you asked your local preacher, he doubtless would point out, by way of rebuttal to the politician and educator, that both Solomon and Lucifer used to hit the canvas with dramatic regularity—the wisest of mortals, the brightest of angels.

(Incidentally and devilishly, "Lucifer" was widely regarded as the name of proud Satan before his fall. Poet John Milton in *Paradise Lost* firmly fixed the name in the English vocabulary. The morning star—bright Venus at dawn—sometimes has been called "Lucifer.")

At risk of turning this into a Sunday sermon, we should note that Thomas Aquinas would qualify his answer to your question by saying that though right reason should lead to morality, the will of man is capable of choosing evil, and the greater the intelligence the greater the evil.

Immanuel Kant, in a Protestant way, would agree with Aquinas and say that there is nothing greater than good will, especially when controlled by reason.

You see, it all depends whom you ask.

When we asked Dr. Miroslav Hanak, a professor of both philosophy and language, he told us about his brilliant cousin who knew 16 languages "but he was a damned liar in all 16." Is it self-serving of Hanak to admit personally knowing only eight languages?

Q: This question concerns capitalization. Is it Platonic or platonic? I read a lot of English literature and see the word printed both ways. Are both of them correct?

Kim Carney
Winnsboro, TX

A: Both of them are correct because they refer to two different things. When written with a capital letter, Platonic refers to a system of philosophy; however, in lower case, it has nothing to do with philosophy but with a friendship between members of the opposite sex—"we're just buddies."

It is understandable that when reading English literature you would find many references to the idealistic philosophical tenets of Plato which, because of his concern for the human spirit and tendency to exalt mind over matter, greatly influenced Shelley and Wordsworth.

In his *Symposium,* Plato tells of the altruistic love of Socrates for young men, basically a search for ideal beauty. Note that at this time, platonic love had nothing to do with members of the opposite sex. However, by 1626 in England, the phrase was applied to similar love between man and woman, and today we frequently hear of a "harmless platonic relationship," play for the boy, tonic for the girl.

Q: During a trivia game, several of the participants referred to the "alligator of the cave." Everybody seemed to know all about this item of common knowledge except me. So next day I asked our science teacher. She didn't know either.

Patti Denman
Cumby, TX

A: What they were talking about was the "Allegory of the Cave," as discussed in Plato's *Republic.* A puppet show is taking place within a cave. But the spectators do not see the show because they are facing the back wall, and, since they are prisoners, they are chained to their benches and cannot turn around. All that they can see are the shadows on the wall, the shadows of the puppets as reflected by the fire in the cave.

The meaning of the allegory, according to most savants, is the intellectual corruption forced upon us by the imprisonment in the body.

Q: I'm looking for a medievalist who can run down two references on the Middle Ages. The first pointed out the high earning power of the average laborer during the Middle Ages. The second one had nothing to do with economics but with the philosophy of Thomas Aquinas. What is the reason for the recent revival of Thomism at the universities? Maybe you have run across it.

Oscar H. Lipscomb
Archbishop of Mobile
Mobile, AL

A: Aquinas was the first to show the logic and reasonableness of the Judaic-Christian theology and way of life. People liked what he taught in the 13th century. Again, in our century they find an emotional reassurance in his teaching, so lucid are his answers, so compelling is his logic.

In an important way, Aquinas offered a better world. He placed man in the center of the universe with a personal God to look after him in this life and point the direction to eternal happiness in the next.

Of course, St. Thomas had the advantage of constructing his philosophy during a relatively stable economic period. The common worker was well paid during much of the Middle Ages. Today when the average worker must labor for 28 weeks to pay for a medium-priced clunker (with a motor tune-up costing about eight and a half hours), he must grimace to learn that medieval man could supply his entire family all its necessities for a year by working only 14 weeks. We are quoting from Professor Thorgold Rogers of Oxford. Another authority, Dr. Werner Sombart, a student of agriculture conditions in Central Europe during the Middle Ages, writes that some communities had as many as 180 holidays a year.

One reason for the revival of Thomism among philosophers is that they have tried everything else. The world view of Aquinas retains a tremendous intellectual appeal.

Many books, old and new, deal with Thomism. But the one passage we found that seemed to encapsulate its most distinctive quality comes from Harvard medievalist Henry Adams (1838–1918) in *Mont-Saint-Michel and Chartres:*

"St. Thomas asked little of man, and gave much; even as much freedom of will as the State gave or now gives; he added immortality hereafter and eternal happiness under reasonable restraints; his God watched over man's temporal welfare far more anxiously than the State has ever done, and assigned him space in the Church which he never can have in the galleries of Parliament or Congress; more than all this, Saint Thomas and his God placed man in the center of the universe, and made the sun and stars for his uses. No statute law ever did as much for man, and no social reform ever will try to do it."

Q: As the campaigns heat up, more and more candidates continue to label the platforms of their opponents as utopian. Is utopian a bad word?

                                        Melinda Underwood
                                        Shawnee, OK

A: Originally the word did not have any pejorative connotation. *Utopia* (1515) was a book about an ideal community, written by a British prime minister, who was both scholar and saint. Although Sir Thomas More wrote the first book in this genre (if we can exclude Plato's *Republic*), there have been many subsequent utopias—where everything is supposed to be good. And there have been *dystopias*—where everything is shown to be bad.

Although utopias afford fascinating reading, each one has the same fundamental error: the author will zero in on one element of society (possibly two), and magnify this particular element while neglecting other values of no less value to society. As a result, the adjective *utopian* has taken on the meaning of *visionary, chimerical, impractical.*

So if your candidate is offering you a pleasant platform of pie in the sky, tax without pain, castles in Spain, you know that it is unquestionably unworkable and utopian.

But Greek scholar Thomas More knew the meaning of the word *utopian* when he brought it into English: *nowhere.*

Q: In your column would you give a simple explanation of the term a priori. *It seems to be in bad repute, especially in literary circles.*

James Ragland
Elysian Fields, TX

A: If there were a God, He would be the greatest being that could be thought of.

But such a being must exist.

Therefore, God exists.

This was the *a priori* reasoning of Anselm back in the 11th century, which continues to tease intellectuals long after Aquinas pointed out its inherent weakness—the transition from the ideal to the real.

As the reader has probably noticed, *a priori* logic moves from cause to effect, from general to particular; over against *a posteriori* which proceeds from effect to cause, from particular to general.

If the derivation is helpful, *a priori* logic means "that which went before," while *a posteriori* means "that which comes after."

More helpful might be an example of *a posteriori* logic, specifically an argument for the existence of a *Prime Mover*. Students of theodicy will recognize this *a posteriori* reasoning as the argument from teleology.

The argument: There are unlimited examples of order and of the striving for order in the universe (the patterns in the solar system, the structure of the atom, the summer solstice, the swallows of Capistrano).

Such an unlimited order argues for an unlimited intelligence. Therefore, this unlimited intelligence is God.

A priori reasoning is deductive; *a posteriori,* inductive. Both were in good repute the last time we checked. What is in bad repute is not *a priori* reasoning but the *apriorism,* a sweeping generalization in which a general rule is applied that doesn't fit all cases.

A priori reasoning certainly is in good repute in the field of mathematics. All geometry proofs, all math proofs, for that matter, are based on *a priori* reasoning. It is also still alive and well in the philosophy of Immanuel Kant, where the term is applied to anything antecedently necessary to make experience intelligible.

Whew.

Q: What is the meaning of scholasticism? I used it for the noun of the adjective scholastic and was informed that scholasticism was a system of philosophy that discussed how many angels could dance on the head of a needle but that it had once been very popular. Is this true?

Barbara Fite
Hughes Springs, TX

A: Scholasticism was a medieval system of philosophy which relied upon Aristotelianism to reconcile the tenets of Christianity with the demands of reason. "Truth cannot contradict truth whether we obtain that truth *immediately* from revelation or *mediately* from the light of reason." Long before the poet's eye would "see the world in a grain of sand and heaven in a wild flower," the mind of Aquinas was demonstrating the existence of God from the argument of motion: "Whatever is moved is moved by something . . . and we must eventually arrive at the concept of the Prime Mover." This was the first reason for the popularity of scholasticism.

The second reason for its popularity was that scholasticism gave clear concise answers to questions that children ask but which adults pooh-pooh as unanswerable ("I—why?" Or: "Who put me here?" Or: "What does it all mean?"), questions so penetrating as to really not be questions at all but requests for emotional assurance. Scholasticism could answer these questions because it was a philosophy of being.

The golden age of scholasticism was the 13th century when, under the leadership of Aquinas and Scotus, the laws of logic and dialectic expanded the frontiers of knowledge. Their successors, however, were satisfied to pedantically quibble over subtleties—such as the number of angels that could dance on the head of a needle—and neglected to look out the window. Outside there was a steam engine. Students of Latin are acquainted with the *Filioque* disputation, the most famous controversy of the Middle Ages. *Filius* is the nominative for *son* while the enclitic *que* means *and*. Did the Holy Ghost proceed from the Father or from the Father *and* the Son? Trivial? Quibbical? It split the Eastern Church from the West!

Q: In Sunday school, which I attend regularly, I learn that God can do everything. Yet at cocktail parties, which I attend with equal regularity, I hear intellectuals dispute His omnipotence with the query: "Can God make something He can't destroy?"
Would you harmonize this seeming contradiction?

Bill Brockman
Dallas, TX

A: "With God all things are possible," according to the first chapter of Luke. According to the *Bible,* there is nothing physically impossible for Him.

But some philosophers contend that He cannot do the metaphysically impossible. And that's what these "intellectuals" may be talking about.

A square circle, for example, cannot exist even in the world of concepts. The *Bible* has something to say on this, if you turn to the sixth chapter, 18th verse of Paul's letter to the Hebrews. It declares that God cannot lie.

A more exhaustive treatment can be found in *Summa Contra Gentiles,* in which Thomas Aquinas discusses the best of possible worlds.

That should interest you since you seem to be enjoying the best of two worlds, cocktail parties and Sunday school.

Q: What is the difference between an atheist and an agnostic; also what is the difference between a "theist" and a "deist," if any?

M. Parris
Mobile, AL

A: Dallasites used to define an *atheist* as a football fan who didn't care who won the Notre Dame-SMU game.

Seriously, an atheist says there is no God; an agnostic says that he doesn't know and that you can't know.

The derivation helps us to understand the meaning. *Theos* is a Greek noun that means *God,* and the *alpha* is a negative: *no God.*

Gignoskein is a Greek verb meaning *to know* and again the *alpha* is negative: *not knowing.*

The English biologist Thomas Henry Huxley is said to have proposed the word *agnostic* at a party in 1869.

Those who believe in a personal God who revealed himself via the Bible are known as *theists*.

Now while Columbus, Copernicus and Galileo were devout theists, their discoveries led to the development of *deism* (from Latin *Deus* for God), the belief in the absentee God, the Great Clockmaker who wound up the clock called the world and walked away, never to be heard from since.

Deism, while etymologically equivalent to theism, is generally defined as that "school of thought which recognizes a personal God but denies His providence or active presence in the life of the world."

The English writers who codified the rules of deism were Edward Herbert and Matthew Tindal, not household names, to be sure, and certainly not as well known as some of the American deists: George Washington, John Adams, Samuel Adams, Alexander Hamilton, and especially Thomas Jefferson and Benjamin Franklin.

Q: Would you explain the difference between the terms classic *and* romantic?

To a student just returning to college after working in the world of reality, these technical terms create quite a problem. Generally when I master a technical term I can recognize it in a fog wearing a disguise, but just after I had pigeon-holed the romantic characteristics of Byron, the professor gleefully explained that the poetry of Byron also has many neo-classic *characteristics.*

Undaunted I started studying the neo-classic characteristics of Alexander Pope. But just when I thought I had mastered them, the same professor smugly began talking about the "many romantic characteristics" of Pope's Windsor Forest.

I wish they would make up their minds. Does a distinction really exist or is this some sort of deal the professors have cooked up so they won't have to go out into the cold world and sell second-rate books? Is that why they have us study so many second-rate writers from the romantic period?

Monica Denny
Greenville, TX

A: Philosophy is at the heart of the dichotomy between *romantic* and *classic* literature. It represents the difference between rule by reason or by emotion, by head or by heart.

Man is basically sinful, according to the classicist, and reason must restrain his passions. To the romanticist, however, a nature boy is basically good and may safely trust his emotions. It's just those artificial institutions that are bad—the noble savage is perfect.

Basically, in graphic arts, the classicist preferred the straight line; the romanticist, curve and color. In music, it was the solid chords of Haydn and Mozart against the cadenzas of Chopin or the sweet sadness of Robert Schumann.

In speaking of English literature, there are, besides the contrast between reason and emotion, other contrasts as well: city versus country, rhymed couplet versus blank verse, and the order of a Greek temple versus the disorder of a Gothic structure.

Of course the characteristics of these two movements intertwined: the classic characteristics were dominant during the first half of the 18th century while the romantic were recessive; then the classic characteristics began to recede during the pre-romantic period from 1750 to 1798 while the romantic began to ascend. Finally, the classic characteristics still continued on, although in a recessive capacity, during the romantic period from 1798 to 1832.

Literature classes often study second-rate writers because they best show the general flavor of an age.

Mediocre writers embody an age; great writers transcend it.

Q: What is Walden *about? Could you tell me in one sentence?*

Jack Trammel
Fort Worth, TX

A: It may take four, counting this one.

Walden is a back-to-nature booklet in which Henry David Thoreau deplores the complicated life of the city and extols the solitude and simplicity one finds in the woods. I won't get into the critics' charge that during his seclusion in the woods, his mother, who lived about a mile away, brought him cookies every Saturday.

Actually, the message of *Walden*—simplify, simplify, simplify—rates imperatively today.

Q: In a psychology class I took with my wife, we were taught that most successful marriages grow out of a relationship that started with a friendship. We passed the course, but we never really did believe it because we liked to believe in love at first sight. Now that we know what the marriage counselors teach, we would like to hear what the literary people say on this subject. Is this what they call courtly love?

Butch Johnson
Carrollton, TX

A: Writers generally go down the line in praise of love at first sight. With them, it is a theme ever-ancient and ever-new. As head-in-the-clouds *Southwest Airlines Magazine* once reported: ". . . It is a fallacy that love develops from long companionship or persevering courtship. Love is an offspring of spiritual affinity, and unless that affinity is created in a moment it will not be created in years."

Love at first sight, no stranger to Chaucer (*Troilus*), perhaps was given its most dramatic exposé by Shakespeare in *As You Like It:* "They no sooner met but they look'd; no sooner look'd but they lov'd; no sooner lov'd but they sigh'd; no sooner sigh'd but they ask'd one another the reason; so sooner knew the reason but they sought the remedy."

Understandably "love at first sight" occurs in French literature and particularly poignantly in Victor Hugo's *Les Miserables:* "Few people dare to say that two beings have fallen in love because they have looked at each other. Yet it is in this way that love begins, and in this way only. The rest is only the rest and comes afterwards. Nothing is more real than these great shocks which two souls give each other in exchanging this spark."

Love at first sight played a role in courtly love—a philosophy of love that existed among the medieval troubadours. In their view, romance was usually accompanied by great emotional disturbances. The lover was bothered and bewildered, emotionally tortured and physically tormented. As for the lady, she was technically unattainable. According to the strictest code of that time, true love was held to be almost impossible in the married state. It was all poetic and unattainable, or, if attainable, illegal.

Why the troubadours felt this way isn't clear, but it probably had something to do with housework.

XV.

The Bible

Q: In the book Things No One Ever Tells You, *I came across a beautiful piece of trivia—Shakespeare may have translated the King James edition of the Bible. "If you check the 46th word from the beginning of Psalm 46, you'll find it is* shake. *Check the 46th word from the end of the psalm and you'll find it's* spear. *The translation of the King James version was completed on William Shakespeare's 46th birthday."*

Would you please comment on this amazing coincidence? Also do scholars know much about Shakespeare's attitude toward religion?

Elke Sommer
Granny's Dinner Playhouse
Dallas, TX

A: Shakespeare certainly believed in prayer. He concluded *The Tempest,* his most autobiographical play, with "my ending is despair unless I be relieved by prayer." No writer was ever more steeped in the otherworldliness of the Middle Ages and few creative writers were more at home in the Bible than he.

But that is just the point: he was too creative to be a reliable translator. "Second-rate writers make better translators," explained Hans Rothe (one of our century's leading translators). Great writers are too subjective, too creative. Schiller's translation of *Macbeth* was bad Schiller and worse Shakespeare.

But there is also internal evidence against the possibility of Shakespeare's having translated the Bible. According to Ben Jonson, Shakespeare had "little Latin and less Greek." And his Hebrew was non-existent. All of the Old Testament was written in Hebrew, including Psalm 46.

Eminent theologian John C. Holbert tells us that the names of the 47 translators of the King James version of the Bible were well documented. Not one of those names was William Shakespeare.

Renaissance scholar Tom Perry hypothesizes that even if Shakespeare did know Hebrew he would not have been conned into this non-profit venture. King James had high praise for the translators but no money. He never gave them a cent. Shakespeare, besides being a creative artist, was also a shrewd businessman. Few, if any, writers made fortunes from their writings before Shakespeare.

Shakespeare's biographers make no mention of his translating. They do point out that during the years 1604–1611, the years covered by King James' venture, our playwright was churning out such monumental works as *Macbeth, Antony & Cleopatra, Coriolanus, Timon of Athens,*

Cymbeline, The Winter's Tale, and *Measure for Measure.* No wonder the "dark lady" of the sonnets deserted him during this busy period. To have taken on another literary task would probably have been unthinkable.

Finally, since Shakespeare was born in 1564, he would have been not 46 in the year 1611 but 47. Alas and alack. The rest is an interesting coincidence.

Q: Please give me the origin of "Jumpin' Jehosofat." I am not even sure of the spelling.

Buddy Wahl
Talco, TX

A: Research revealed five biblical characters with the name of *Jehoshaphat,* none of whom was noted for levitation, resilience, or any unusual athletic prowess—not even King Jehoshaphat, the son of Asa.

"Jumpin' Jehosaphat" is in the same category as "Gee Whiz" and other euphemisms: compromises between the urge to cuss and the desire to be inoffensive. Historians of profanity tell us that "Jumpin' Jehosaphat" developed during the middle part of the 19th century and became immediately popular because the consonant combinations enabled the cusser to sustain and elaborate long rhetorical rolls.

The purpose of profanity—and euphemisms for profanity—is to offer emotional release, and the more elaborate the rhetorical roll, the faster the relief. "Jumpin' H. Jehosaphat," for example, gives even faster relief.

Q: Would you please comment on the following two items:

Item one: The National Council of Churches, in order to eliminate sexist references in the Bible, is planning to adapt certain portions of the Holy Book, at least those portions read in public. Thus "God the Father" will emerge as "God the Creator," and similar changes will be made with all references to Jesus, the Holy Spirit, and human beings. The solicitude of the Council proceeds from "complaints by women that a cultural bias (pervades) in both the Bible and worship services."

Item two: The National Council of Teachers of English has recommended the use of plural pronouns as acceptable for masculine singular when the indefinite pronoun is concerned. "Anyone who wants to go to the game should bring their money tomorrow . . ." would be just as

acceptable as "Anyone who wants to go to the game, should bring his
money tomorrow . . ."
We would like to see this discussed.

Dr. Blanche Jamison
Durant, OK

A: Item one: etymologists tell us that merely changing "God the Father"
to "God the Creator" will not remove the masculinity—it would have to be
"God the Creating Person" or "God the Creating Committee"—because
the enclitic "—or" is just as masculine as "Father." Neither is every student
of exegesis in agreement since the nouns in question are clearly spelled out
as "father" and "son" in Hebrew, Greek and Latin (the Greek word for
"spirit," however, is neuter). If they fudge in this instance, how long will
their readers accept the Bible as the gospel truth?

Item two: Here too we noted a lack of unanimity among the specialists
and strong opposition from teachers of foreign languages.

"How can we tell the student that a pronoun must agree with its antecedent in gender and number when you tell him (or *them*) that it doesn't?
Foreign language is hard enough as it is. Why confuse them?"

Another possibility would be to accept the generic pronoun formulated
by a committee: *tey, ter, tem.* "The IRS expects every American to pay *ter*
just share until *tey* dies or it will punish *tem.*"

"The history of languages shows that, while new words may catch on
overnight, changes in grammar generally require more than a century and
novel suggestions in grammar are always met with passive resistance by
the populace. Thank God.

Q: In a play by Tennessee Williams, the verb know *has an unusual conno-*
tation: to imply sexual intimacy, something like "he knew her in the Bibli-
cal sense of the word." Frequently in the Bible we read about "four hundred
young virgins who had never known men." My question is whether this
is a special Hebrew verb, or did the idea of cohabitation come from the
context?
It was Tennessee Williams, wasn't it?

Randall Cobb
Abilene, TX

A: The passage you speak of occurs in the third scene of *Summer And*
Smoke. "He knew the Gonzales girl, all right, in the Biblical sense of
the word."

There are four Hebrew verbs for *know. Yada* is the one in question, and it occurs 735 times. Generally it performs such routine function as "Noah *knew* that the flood waters had abated," or "I *know* that thou fearest God." On fourteen occasions sex appears, but it is always in the context of the sentence, as in Genesis 4:1—"And Adam *knew* Eve his wife; and she conceived, and bore Cain, and said, I have gotten a man from the Lord," and Numbers 31:17—"Now therefore kill every male among the little ones, and kill every woman that hath *known* man by lying with him."

Q: Who applied the term "The Golden Rule" to the famous words of Jesus in Matthew 7:12 and Luke 6:31?

Marguerite Miller
Vernon, TX

A: The oldest known use of the term "The Golden Rule" that we could locate was in 1542 when it was used in the field of mathematics and was also called "The Rule of Three."

As to the biblical exhortation, it was called "The Golden Law" in 1674; "The Golden Principle" in 1741; and "The Golden Rule" in 1807 in *The Medical Journal.* But there is more to it than this.

We must remember that during the Middle Ages every alchemist was in search of the philosopher's stone, a stone that could transmute base metal into gold, for gold was considered the perfect metal. It was but natural that this perfect rule would eventually bear the appellation of the perfect metal, long before it was recorded in the references just cited.

Q: Some of our tech writers are having trouble with a *and* an. *According to the King James Version of the Bible, you're supposed to use* a *before consonants,* an *before vowels. One would think that if the King James Version of the Bible was good enough for Christ it would be good enough for the rest of us, but one sees an awful lot of inconsistencies.*

Virginia Carroll
Garland, TX

A: The issue hinges on the difference between orthography and sound. The rule isn't just "*a* before consonants and *an* before vowels" but *a* before a consonant sound and *an* before a vowel sound. We should emphasize the word *sound* in each instance.

Although it brought problems to Eve, none of us have any trouble with "an apple" or even with "an only child," and the more corpulent of us can deal with "a middleweight" or even with "a heavyweight." But everyone of us has had trouble with "an honest man" or "an heir apparent." The problem arises because with both *honest* and *heir* (as with *hour* and *honor*) the letter *h* is silent; we are now dealing with a vowel sound and the article *an* must be used: "an hour ago" or "an hour bestowed." American English is quite consistent in this instance. On the other hand if a word begins with a vowel that has a consonant sound (*unique* has a *you* sound), then we employ the article *a:* "a eulogy to remember" or "a useful operation," etc.

True it is that the Bible consistently used *an* before *h:* "Pleasant words are as an honeycomb . . . An hypocrite shall not come before . . . They had sung an hymn." But in the days of King James, the letter *h* was not pronounced in these words. The rule hasn't changed; only the pronunciation.

When in doubt as to whether to use *a* or *an,* read it aloud. Your ear is your best guide.

Q: I read the Bible a lot, and though the "Good Book" is generally easy to follow, there's one expression that puzzles me: "the apple of his eye." The first time I read that I thought of William Tell. Then I began to wonder whether Moses was speaking about a part of his eye or about the apple that he had his eye on?

Larry Mahan
Phoenix, AZ

A: You can bet your boots it refers to the eyeball.

Since the pupil of the eye had been called the *apple* way back in Anglo-Saxon times, it was most normal for the translator to render his expression as "apple of the eye." especially when the Latin word was *pupilla.*

In the original Hebrew it was *ishon,* which meant *a little man.* The commentators immediately assure us, however, that *ishon* means the pupil of the eye since it is the part of the eye where the onlooker may see his image reflected in miniature.

Q: Is there any special reason why the cartilage in the throat is called the Adam's apple? Does it have the same name in foreign countries?

Lisa Deckert
Deer Park, TX

A: According to a pious superstition, Adam changed his mind when the apple was halfway down and tried to cough it out. He was unsuccessful, however, and a bite of that apple grew into a cartilage to become the Adam's apple.

The legend apparently spread throughout Europe, for in German it became *Adamsapfel,* which pattern recurs in all the Romance and Slavic languages. In China, however, they call this cartilage a *crystal.*

Going back to Adam, we note that he held three distinctions: the first man to live like a man, the first man to love like a man, and the first man to take adversity like a man—blaming it on a woman.

Q: We had a new preacher last Sunday who quoted a passage from the Bible about "gilding the lily." I looked for it but could find it in none of the Bible concordances. Can you help? Besides giving me the source of this ancient expression, could you also give the origin of the modern expression "right on?" He employed that one, too, but very tactfully and reverently.

Ms. Brenda Haley
Mount Vernon, TX

A: Don't lose confidence in your ability as a researcher since the expression comes not from the Bible but from Shakespeare's *King John.* The quotation is "To gild refined gold, to paint the lily . . . is wasteful and ridiculous excess." The other expression, often associated with the black civil rights movement and once accompanied by a raised right arm, may also date back to Shakespeare. The young Roman speaker is Mark Antony: "I only speak right on." Shakespeare is ever ancient and ever new. Right on.